HOW
CAN
I
FORGIVE?

David –
Thanks for
your gifts &
leadership –
God's blessing
and grace,

[signature]

HOW CAN I FORGIVE?

A Study of Forgiveness

FaithQuestions SERIES

Joretta L. Marshall

ABINGDON PRESS
NASHVILLE

How Can I Forgive?
A Study of Forgiveness

Scripture quotations in this publication, unless otherwise indicated, are from the New Revised Standard Version of the Bible, copyright © 1989, by the Division of Christian Education of the National Council of the Churches of Christ in the United States of America, and are used by permission.

This book is printed on acid-free, elemental chlorine-free paper.

ISBN: 0-687-05461-3

05 06 07 08 09 10 11 12 13 14 —10 9 8 7 6 5 4 3 2 1

MANUFACTURED IN THE UNITED STATES OF AMERICA

CONTENTS

HOW TO USE
HOW CAN I FORGIVE?
A STUDY OF FORGIVENESS

HOW CAN I FORGIVE? invites the reader to explore the process of forgiveness as a way to deepen connections with God, self, and neighbor. The book is designed for use in any of three settings: 1) adult Sunday school; 2) weekday adult groups; and 3) retreat settings. It can also provide a meaningful resource for private study.

Sunday School: HOW CAN I FORGIVE? may be used on Sunday mornings as a short-term, seven-week study. Sunday morning groups generally last 45 to 60 minutes. If your group would like to go into greater depth, you can divide the chapters and do the study for longer than seven weeks.

Weekday Study: If you use HOW CAN I FORGIVE? in a weekday study, we recommend 90-minute sessions. Participants should prepare ahead by reading the content of the chapter and choosing one activity for deeper reflection and study. A group leader may wish to assign these activities.

Retreat Study: You may wish to use HOW CAN I FORGIVE? in a more intense study, like a weekend retreat. Distribute the books at least two weeks in advance. Locate and provide additional media resources and reference materials, such as Bible dictionaries and commentaries. Tell participants to read HOW CAN I FORGIVE? before the retreat begins. Begin on Friday with an evening meal or refreshments followed by gathering time and worship. Discuss Chapter 1. Cover Chapters 2, 3, 4, and 5 on Saturday and Chapters 6 and 7 on Sunday. Develop a schedule that includes time for breaks, meals, and personal reflection of various topics in the chapters. End the retreat with closing worship on Sunday afternoon.

Leader/Learner Helps

Leader/learner helps are located in boxes near the relevant main text. They include a variety of discussion and reflection activities. Include both the gathering and closing worship activities in each session of your study, and choose from among the other leader/learner helps to fit the time frame you have chosen for your group.

The activities in the leader/learner helps meet the needs of a variety of personalities and ways of learning. They are designed to stimulate both solitary reflection and group discussion. An interactive and informal environment will foster a dynamic interchange of ideas and demonstrate the value of diverse perspectives. While the readings may be done in the group, reading outside of the session will enrich individual reflection and group discussion.

The Role of the Group Leader

The group leader facilitates the gathering and closing worship, organizes the group for each session, monitors the use of time so that adequate attention is given to all major points of the chapter, and encourages an atmosphere of mutual respect and Christian caring. The leader should participate fully in the study as both learner and leader. The same person may lead all the sessions, or each session may have a different leader.

INTRODUCTION

As human beings, our lives are knit together with the pain and agony of suffering, the honest struggle of repentance, and the joy of experiencing the grace of a God whose forgiveness extends beyond the boundaries of our imagination and whose spirit encourages us to live as forgiven and forgiving people. Forgiveness is one of the central tenets of the Christian faith, and it touches the very core of our human existence as we relate to ourselves, to one another, to communities, and to God. Think about the ways the struggle of forgiveness plays a part in our lives.

• On Sunday morning, we say the Lord's Prayer as a community and repeat the words "Forgive us our trespasses, as we forgive those who trespass against us." We participate in the service of the Lord's Supper. There we are met with the words "You are forgiven." We hear the words of Jesus on the cross, saying, "Forgive them; for they do not know what they are doing" (Luke 23:34).
• A teenager in the congregation is involved in a serious traffic accident, and one of her best friends is killed. After several months, she still is unable to talk about the experience. Her pastor has suggested to her that she needs to forgive herself. The young woman thinks she will never be able to do that. Or perhaps it would be more accurate to say that she doesn't feel she deserves to be forgiven.
• An adult woman who attends church faithfully and takes on leadership within the community is encouraged to forgive her uncle for the sexual abuse she experienced when she was a child. Yet, she wonders if such forgiveness is ever possible. A well-meaning family friend suggests that she forget about what happened to her so long ago and move on with her life.
• A family watches as the patriarch of the family dies a slow and painful death from a debilitating disease. One of the daughters of the elderly man says to her sister during a vigil at his bedside that she will

never forgive God for letting this disease ravage her father's body. Her sister is stunned and immediately suggests that God is in control of life and death, and God should not be questioned. She tells her sister that she must ask for forgiveness from God for her thoughts.

• A church is torn by conflict over a social issue that confronts the denomination. In the process of significant debate on the issue, people begin to speak out of their deep passions. The debate appears to be rather calm on the outside, yet people experience dismissal and hurt throughout. Best friends are now on opposite sides of the issue, and the conflict seems to be creating more pain as the days go by. Some are threatening to leave the church; others just want people to forgive for the sake of peace in the church.

Each of these vignettes illustrates the struggle to address issues of forgiveness. We understand it to be a concept central to the Christian tradition, yet we also know it is one of the most difficult processes we face as individuals and as communities. Without forgiveness, we are left with lives consumed by our angers, hurts, and pains. We also know that forgiveness offered too quickly without appropriate repentance and change does not lead us to wholeness. When we live our lives as forgiven and forgiving people, we change the relationships of which we are a part, and ultimately the world around us is affected as well.

Yet, what precisely do we mean when we talk about forgiveness? How does one forgive one's self, another human being, or a community? What is God's role in the forgiveness process? What gets in our way when we want to forgive? What resources can we draw upon in the process of forgiveness?

This study on forgiveness invites us to use our minds, souls, experiences, and feelings to wrestle with a process that can lead us to deeper connections to God, self, and others. Drawing upon the resources of our biblical tradition, the gifts of theology, and the insights from our life experiences, we will examine the process of forgiveness.

A word of caution is in order as we begin. Thinking about and reflecting upon forgiveness often touches past wounds and injuries in our emotional, physical, or spiritual world. Be gentle with one another in this study. Ask questions carefully, and listen to one another deeply. Invite God's daily presence into the process. Take care of yourselves, and care about one another, knowing that God desires us to live holy and whole lives. Pray with one another, and pray for those whom you do not know who are carrying pain or experiencing harm and for whom forgiveness feels distant. Receive the gift of forgiveness, and offer it generously with care.

Acknowledgements

Writing about forgiveness is impossible without the grace and wisdom of friends, colleagues, students, and church members who are willing to share their insights, questions, and stories of the faithful struggle to forgive. Thanks to the many churches who have invited me to offer classes on forgiveness and to those who have shared their stories of pain and healing in the process. Faculty colleagues at Iliff School of Theology and Eden Theological Seminary, students who participated in a class on forgiveness and pastoral care in the fall of 2004, and colleagues in the American Association of Pastoral Counselors have all provided insights into this project and helped hone my understandings. I am grateful for the support and help of Chris Davis, who managed to keep my administrative calendar clear so I could take time for writing. Karen Farthing, a graduate of Eden Seminary, not only tracked down resources but read and commented on drafts of this material. I was blessed with a capable and generous editor, Pamela Dilmore, who invited me into the process and encouraged me along the way. My family continues to teach me about the importance of gentle care and grace in the midst of living. For the presence of Joy, Hope, Dana, and Grace—all who received less daily attention than they should while I was writing—I am deeply thankful. This work is dedicated to the memory of my father, Jimmie, and his sister, Arlene, who continue to live in my soul as saints of the faith.

CHAPTER 1
BIBLICAL INSIGHTS
ON FORGIVENESS

Focus: The biblical witness tells us that forgiveness is a gift from God that works to restore our relationships with the Holy One and with one another. Just as God extends forgiveness to us, we are called to forgive others.

Gathering

Read Psalm 51:1-2. Reflect on a personal dilemma in your life, in the life of a friend or family member, or in the life of the world. What do these words from the psalmist say to you? Give thanks for the gift of forgiveness. Pray together the following prayer: "God of hope, love, and new life, as we move through this study, there will be many times when issues of forgiveness and the stories that are shared will have an impact on our personal lives. Help us to be aware of places of pain, sadness, hope, fear, anger, or grace. Help us to be gentle with ourselves and with one another. Open our hearts and minds throughout the course of this study to the work of forgiveness in our lives. In Christ we pray. Amen."

Christianity Teaches Forgiveness

Faithful Christians in every family, church, and community wrestle with issues of forgiveness on a daily basis. We wonder what it means to forgive in situations like these:

• A young woman struggles to forgive her mother for abandoning her as a child.

• A couple files for divorce after it was discovered that one of them had an affair.

• A pastor in a neighboring congregation is accused of embezzling money from the church.

• An elementary school student riding his bike is struck by a teen-age driver.

• A soldier kills someone from "the other side" and wonders what kind of family the man leaves behind.

• Members of a local church leave because they are tired of the "hypocrites" in the church whom they cannot forgive.

We seek to forgive because we believe it to be a central tenet of our faith. As Christians, we turn to the Bible for guidance and insight about what the forgiveness of God means in our lives. We wonder what to do in situations where we feel wronged or how to restore relationships when we have wronged others. We believe the mandate of Scripture is not only to ask for forgiveness but to offer it to others as well. From Old Testament accounts of God's establishing a covenant with the people to New Testament convictions about the role of forgiveness in the Christian life, it is clear that this concept is central to a life of faith.

As we examine the texts about forgiveness, we come to deeper under-standings of forgiveness, its meaning, and its moral imperative on our lives. Both through the examination of specific texts where forgiveness is a cen-tral claim and an exploration of overarching themes found in the Scriptures, we gain insight into what forgiveness means for our daily living.

Hebrew and Greek Words

In an effort to understand more fully the meaning of the word *forgive-ness*, it is helpful to return to the Hebrew and Greek language and examine the terms in their earlier forms. Words that are later translated as "forgive," "forgiveness," or "forgiven" appear over 150 times in the New Revised Standard Version of the Scripture. As one scholar notes, "the vocabulary of forgiveness is complex and rich in both the Hebrew and the Greek."[1]

Over twenty different Hebrew and Greek words are used in the Old Testament for forgiveness, and each one carries multiple layers of mean-ing. The etymology, or derivation, of these words suggests such meanings as "to cover over," "to send away," "to pardon," "to remove," "to make atonement," "to overlook intentionally," "to be merciful," "to go unpunished," or "to hold guiltless." The vocabulary associated with forgiveness points toward the restoration of the broken relationship between God and humans. Through forgiveness, God removes the barriers that keep us from fully experiencing God's abundance.[2] From the stories of Creation through the covenants established with Noah, Moses, and David to the journey of the exiles and the Exodus, forgiveness offers ways for the sins of the people to be covered over, atoned, or pardoned.

Fewer Greek words are used in the New Testament to articulate notions of forgiveness, but their connotations are similar to those in the Old Testament. Terms related to forgiveness carry meanings such as "to send away," "to permit," "to release from bondage," "not to hinder," "to leave," "to go away from one in order to go to another place," "to give up a debt," and "to keep no longer."[3] As with those words used in the Old Testament, the etymology of the Greek New Testament words is nuanced in ways that suggest something unique about forgiveness. Ultimately, the power of forgiveness is that it removes or releases us from sin in ways that free us to pursue right relationships with one another, with ourselves, with the community around us, and with God. From the life and ministry of Jesus through the Acts of the Apostles and those who followed the Christ, forgiveness is a central theme in the New Testament.

From a biblical perspective, forgiveness rests as one of the pivotal marks of the Christian life. Through the language of the Scriptures, we find indications of the power of forgiveness as it is offered by God and as those who would follow Christ are admonished to forgive one another and to live the life of forgiveness.

Themes Related to Forgiveness

The Scriptures offer us rich and complex ways of understanding and thinking about forgiveness, its importance, and its power. While it is impossible to do a comprehensive biblical study in the limited space of this study, it is

Five Biblical Themes
1. God offers forgiveness.
2. God holds us accountable for our sins but does not hold us hostage.
3. Repentance is a significant aspect of forgiveness.
4. We are to live as forgiven and forgiving people.
5. God seeks justice, reconciliation, and wholeness.

important to explore some of the understandings found in the Scriptures. Five themes related to forgiveness assist us in understanding a biblical foundation for forgiveness in our lives.

God Offers Forgiveness

Over and over again in the Scriptures, we are told that forgiveness is something that God offers to human beings and to the world; it is not something that we create or sustain on our own. Forgiveness is ultimately the work of God. In response to our human sin, God provides a way for us to restore our primary connection to the Holy One. In the Hebrew texts, God's offer of forgiveness is tied to the covenant established with the people. It is upon the foundations of this covenant that we come to understand our relationship with God, our need for forgiveness, and God's generous offer of steadfast love in response.

The establishment of the covenants with Noah, Moses, David, Solomon, and the Israelite community are signs of God's love and grace offered to all of creation. The covenant is more than a promise by God that the Israelite people would thrive and live securely in the land; rather, the covenant is the formation of a specific kind of relationship between the people and God. The relationship is built on the mercy and steadfast love of God. Laws, rules, and norms are established to protect the relationship and to maintain justice and peace in the household

> Read Psalm 106:43-45 and Matthew 26:26-29. What do these Scriptures say to you about God's role in the process of forgiveness? What other thoughts or ideas about forgiveness do you see in these Scriptures?

of God. What is important to focus on is not the specific rules and laws that are noted. Instead, the function of the rules is to keep the relationship between God and humans holy. God's desire is that we live holy lives. The rules become a means toward that end. It has been noted that "the rupture of covenant between the soul and God and the people of [the] covenant is something more personal and spiritual than breaking the rules. It is the destruction of a quality of life we call holy."[4]

As has always been the case, humans are "stiff-necked people" who challenge God and who break the covenants. Hence, there was a need for God to create a way for the people to return to or to restore their right relationship with God. God's desire for people to live a holy life is constantly

16

met by the mercy of forgiveness as it operates to restore our relationship with God, with one another, and with all creation.

The steadfastness of God's forgiveness is poignantly illustrated in the stories of the Exodus. As the people find themselves lost and afraid in the desert, they begin to grumble and test Moses and God. They challenge Moses, asking why they were brought into the desert to die when they at least knew what they were facing at home. Moses intercedes on their behalf, and God provides for them in spite of their grumbling (Exodus 16:2-4; 17:2-7). This story in the Hebrew Scriptures reminds those who hear that God is "slow to anger, and abounding in steadfast love" (Exodus 34:6). The rehearsal of the people breaking covenant and God extending forgiveness is told throughout the Old Testament, encouraging listeners to claim deep in their souls that God is the one who forgives and who walks with them through the desert, keeping covenant with them throughout the journey (Exodus 34:1-9; 2 Chronicles 7:12-22; Psalm 106).

> Read Exodus 34:1-9 and 2 Chronicles 7:12-22. What relationships do you see between God's covenant with the people and forgiveness? How do these Scriptures inform contemporary Christian life?

We know that the covenant was not established solely for the sake of the communities of the Old Testament, nor was forgiveness central only to the God of the Hebrew Scriptures. Forgiveness continues to play a dominant role in the New Testament and is embodied in the works and ministry of Christ and those who follow him. We are told that Jesus established a new covenant. The symbols of our communion with God can be found in the body and blood of Jesus Christ and the sacrament we celebrate in remembrance of Christ (Matthew 26:26-29). On behalf of God, Jesus offers forgiveness freely for those in need of healing (Mark 2:1-12). Even at the point of agony on the cross, Jesus asked God to forgive those who were

> Form teams of three. Read Mark 2:1-12. What does this Scripture say to you about the connections between healing and forgiveness? What implications do these connections have in contemporary life? Read aloud Acts 5:31, Colossians 1:13-14, and Ephesians 1:7. How do these Scriptures speak to you about God's work of forgiveness through Jesus Christ?

persecuting him and presumably offered God's forgiveness for the thief who hung beside him (Luke 23:32-43). The Acts of the Apostles and the writers of the letters pick up the theme by reminding people that God forgives (Acts 5:31; Colossians 1:13-14; Ephesians 1:7).

God makes covenant with the people of God, offering them laws and rules to make their relationships with God and with one another full of holiness and goodness. Humans fall short in living holy lives, and we fracture the covenant. Forgiveness is God's gift, inviting us back into right relationship with God, with one another, with our community and world, and with ourselves.

God Holds Us Accountable for Our Sins But Does Not Hold Us Hostage

With astounding clarity, the Scriptures confirm for us two paradoxical things. First and foremost, we have a God who is steadfast in mercy and love. As mentioned earlier, Exodus 34 reminds us that God is a God of immeasurable grace, "slow to anger, and abounding in steadfast love and faithfulness" (v. 6). Yet, secondly we are reminded that just as God's mercy visits generation after generation, the sins of one generation carry over to the next in some manner. This represents the paradox of our belief in a God whose mercy is everlasting and who, at the same time, does not simply ignore our human failures.[5]

This paradox is seen in the earliest Creation stories of Genesis. The stories suggest that God's creativity and mark on the world are to be seen as good. At the same time, the humans created in the image of God make choices that result in their banishment from the garden. The texts in Genesis 1 and 2 remind us that God is a compassionate and creating God, yet God is also one who holds us accountable for our actions and sins. Many stories in the Hebrew texts bring to mind the power of a God who offers choice and free will to human beings, and they in turn are held accountable for their sins and wrongdoings. The humans are banished from the garden, the people of the Exodus are told that the sins of the parents would visit the children for generations to come, and we are reminded that whole communities in the Hebrew Scriptures are destroyed because they did not follow God's commands.

The good news is that God holds deeper wells of mercy than our sin can ever reach. What we glimpse is the work of a God who is willing to take a risk on those of us called to be the children of God. With the risk of freedom comes the undeniable struggle to live in human relationships where we also cause grief to God because of our actions. Stories in the Old and New Testament are filled with this paradox of being held accountable and, at the same time, met with the grace and

> Read Luke 15 and Matthew 18:23-35. What do these parables say to you about God? About human beings? About forgiveness?

mercy of a forgiving God. Jesus reminds the listeners in various parables that God is both the one who looks for the lost (Luke 15) and the one who seeks justice and rightness (Matthew 18:23-35).

Human beings, created both in the image of God and filled with the vulnerabilities of sin and disobedience, provide ample opportunity for God to hold us accountable. Whether wandering in the desert and crying out about the unfairness of being brought this far only to find ourselves without the resources we think we need, or whether we are paralyzed by our sins in ways that keep us from experiencing healing, we are still held accountable for our disobedience, and God meets us with mercy.

Repentance Is a Significant Aspect of God's Forgiveness

In order for the process of forgiveness to be complete, the biblical texts often suggest that particular actions on the part of humans are required. Our sins are covered over, atoned for, or released from debt by God, but humans are asked to be honest and forthright in approaching God. In Hebrew, the word for *repent* suggests the notion of "turning" or "returning" to God. The Greek word translated as *repent* suggests "to think differently" or "to reconsider." In light of the grace of God's steadfast love and mercy, we respond to our failures as human beings through activities of sacrifice, offering, and repentance. As we "turn" to God, we discover the gift of forgiveness.

> Form two teams. Team one should read 1 Kings 8:46-53, and team two should read Luke 3:1-6. What is the context for the word *repent* in the Scripture? What is going on? What does *repentance* mean in the Scripture? How does the Scripture inform your understanding of repentance?

The early Hebrew texts included many instructions about the kinds of sacrifices required to "atone" for the sins of the people. Atonement becomes the way that God restores right relationships with the people. The rituals offered opportunities for the worshipers to approach God and to seek forgiveness or atonement for their sins. Offering animals that were "clean" was a way for the people to bring themselves before God, trusting that God's mercy would be shown. A spirit of penitence, as noted in the Psalms, admonished people to come before God with honesty and forthrightness (Psalm 51). Through ritual sacrifices, the people approached God with contrite and pure hearts, appeasing God and finding ways to restore their relationship with the Holy One and with one another (see Leviticus 4 and 5, for example).

We are reminded that "sacrifice is not the purchase of forgiveness but the claiming of God's promise of mercy."[6] Solomon reminds the people in the establishment of the temple that repentance is connected to the worship of a God who is merciful (2 Chronicles 6:36-42). Those in charge of the temple and the worship life of the community become keepers of the rituals that lead the people back to God through sacrifice, repentance, and forgiveness.

Building upon the Old Testament, the writers of the New Testament continue an emphasis on sacrifice, atonement, and repentance as part of the forgiveness process. Early in the Gospel stories, the words of John the Baptist call people to repentance and the forgiveness of sins. Such repentance plays a significant role in Jesus'

Look up the words *sacrifice* and *atonement* in a Bible dictionary. How does your research inform your understanding of the experiences of repentance and forgiveness through rituals of worship?

ministry. While it is true that Jesus does not always ask people first to repent before he offers healing, he does send them forth with words such as "Your sins are forgiven" (Matthew 9:2; Luke 7:48). The parables of the lost coin, the lost sheep, and the prodigal son remind us that God celebrates those who repent (Luke 15). Peter later reminds the early converts that they are to "repent, and be baptized" (Acts 2:38).

Notions of sacrifice, atonement, and repentance are abundant in the Scriptures. In our most traditional theological understandings, we understand that Jesus becomes the sacrifice and atonement for our sins, restoring our relationship with God. Forgiveness is offered through the saving work of Christ. From other theological perspectives, we recognize that individual and communal repentance becomes our honest response to God and to one another in light of our sins and wrongdoings. In this way, we participate in moving toward wholeness and holiness as people who are forgiven.

We Are to Live as Forgiven and Forgiving People

While we know that forgiveness has a significant place in the stories of the Bible, we wonder at times how appropriate these stories are in our everyday lives. Even if we come to know and believe that we are forgiven by God, what difference does that make in our living? The Scriptures offer us insight into the call of God not only to accept that we are forgiven but also to live as people who practice the art of forgiveness in our relationships with others.

The invitation to live as *forgiven* and *forgiving* people suggests two things at once. First, to live as forgiven people means to accept the mercy and grace of a God whose love is steadfast. God's abundance in terms of grace is always sufficient for our needs. Psalm 99 encourages us to give thanks to God for the gift of forgiveness. As people of God, we embrace the knowledge that we are a forgiven people, both as individuals and as a community. At the same time, it is not enough to rest in the grace of forgiveness for ourselves without practicing that forgiveness in our relationships with others.

> What situations might impede or block the call to be gracious and generous with our forgiveness?

Hence, the second reality we face is that our experience of forgiveness becomes the foundation from which we live as new creatures in the world. As such, we are called to live in fellowship and grace with one another. Through a covenant established with God, alongside the saving work of Jesus Christ and with the power of the Holy Spirit, we are called to be gracious and generous with our forgiveness.

While stories in the Old Testament can be found that illustrate the importance of forgiving one another (the story of Joseph and his brothers in Genesis 50:15-21, for example), it is in the Gospels and Epistle writings where we find the clearest indications that we are to live as people who

> Form three teams. Team one should read Genesis 50:15-21, team two should read Matthew 6:9-15, and team three should read Ephesians 4:31–5:2. How do these Scriptures inform your understanding of the need to forgive?

21

forgive one another. There are many parables that invite the listeners to contemplate what it means to forgive one another. For instance, the prodigal son wanders away from home and is welcomed back by his father, forgiven for his arrogance (Luke 15:11-32). In the parable of the unforgiving servant, Jesus comments on the significance of mercy and forgiveness (Matthew 18:23-35). The disciples are admonished to forgive so that God can also forgive them (Mark 11:25). The Lord's Prayer includes a command to forgive others just as we are forgiven (Matthew 6:9-14). Likewise, the Letters of the New Testament contain numerous directions to practice forgiveness with one another (2 Corinthians 2:5-8; Colossians 3:13; Ephesians 4:31-32; James 5:15-16).

Not only are we told to forgive, but we are also encouraged to forgive in endless fashion; forgiveness is to be part and parcel of our daily Christian life. In Matthew 18:21-22, Peter asks Jesus how often he must forgive others. The response from Jesus is to forgive seventy-seven times—a number that suggests completeness. We are to forgive until the forgiveness is whole. There is an important caveat to remember in this text. While we are encouraged to practice the art of forgiveness in our daily relationships, we are not to confuse this with allowing relationships that are harmful and destructive to control our lives. The process of forgiveness is sometimes long as we seek wholeness in our relationships. In fact, in the story of Joseph and his brothers, we have a biblical model for the process of forgiveness requiring time. It took Joseph a while to get to the point of forgiving his brothers for what they did to him (Genesis 45:1-15).

God Seeks Justice, Reconciliation, and Wholeness

Justice and mercy are partners in this process of forgiveness. We are called not to worship our relationships but to live faithfully and as honestly as possible. To live as forgiven people compels us to practice the art of forgiveness with others. "Forgiveness as it is expressed in Jesus' prayer…is not a status one achieves; it is rather a life into which one enters."[7] In the next session, we will examine more fully how forgiveness is connected to God's desire for justice, reconciliation, wholeness, and holiness. There are many who would suggest that the ultimate goal of forgiveness in the Scriptures is to lead us toward reconciliation with God and with one another.[8] While reconciliation is indeed central to the gospel claim, it should not be seen as the only reason for such things as repentance and forgiveness. Instead, forgiveness is part of a larger vision that God has for the community of faith, for the world, and for creation.

What is clear is that the reign of God will include acts of forgiveness, reconciliation, hope, love, and justice. Forgiveness becomes one avenue toward that larger vision of God's world of *shalom* (peace). As forgiven and forgiving people, our energy and focus are renewed, and we find new ways of working toward justice, reconciliation, and wholeness. Ultimately, this is the call of the children of God.

Closing Worship
Give thanks for God's gift of forgiveness and steadfast love. Pray that God will bless each one this week as we reach out as forgiving people. Close by praying together the Lord's Prayer.

For Further Reading
Forgiveness, Reconciliation, and Moral Courage: Motives and Designs for Ministry in a Troubled World, by Robert L. Browning and Roy A. Reed (William B. Eerdmans Publishing Company, 2004).
Forgiveness and Abuse: Jewish and Christian Reflections, edited by Marie M. Fortune and Joretta L. Marshall (Haworth Pastoral Press, 2003).

Notes

[1] From "Forgiveness and Reconciliation," by R. W. Yarbrough, in *New Dictionary of Biblical Theology,* edited by T. Desmond Alexander and Brian S. Rosner (InterVarsity Press, 2000); page 499.

[2] From "Forgiveness," by W. A. Quanbeck, in *The Interpreter's Dictionary of the Bible,* Vol. 2, edited by George Arthur Buttrick (Abingdon Press, 1962); page 315.

[3] From "Forgiveness"; page 315.

[4] From *Forgiveness, Reconciliation, and Moral Courage: Motives and Designs for Ministry in a Troubled World,* by Robert L. Browning and Roy A. Reed (William B. Eerdmans Publishing Company, 2004); page 82.

[5] From *Forgiveness, Reconciliation, and Moral Courage: Motives and Designs for Ministry in a Troubled World;* pages 76–77.

[6] From "Forgiveness"; page 316.

[7] From *Forgiveness, Reconciliation and Moral Courage: Motives and Designs for Ministry in a Troubled World;* page 93.

[8] From "Forgiveness and Reconciliation"; page 502.

CHAPTER 2
THEOLOGICAL INSIGHTS
ON FORGIVENESS

Focus: To understand forgiveness, we must wrestle with theological concepts such as sin, justice, reconciliation, and wholeness. Through the gift of forgiveness, God intends to restore right relationships.

Gathering

Greet one another. As you arrive, help create a group mural by writing about or drawing sketches about ways that forgiveness relates to the theological concepts of sin, justice, reconciliation, and wholeness. Talk with one another about what you have written or drawn. Pray together the following prayer: "God of all people, help us as we explore what it means to experience justice, reconciliation, and wholeness through the process of forgiveness. In the power of your forgiving love, we pray. Amen."

Case Study

Michael has been a member of the same church for thirty years. He and his wife, Sheila, adopted an infant about two years ago. As a child, Michael's father and mother divorced when it was discovered that his mother was having an affair with another man. After the divorce, Michael's father relocated to a distant city in order to secure a job promotion. Michael lived with his mother and stepfather. He is currently feeling anger toward Sheila because she seems to be abandoning him emotionally just as his job is in jeopardy through corporate downsizing. Michael spends much time and energy feeling anger and hurt. This past Sunday in church, the sermon was on forgiveness, and the Lord's Supper was cele-

> What is forgiveness for Michael? Whom does he need to forgive? Are there things for which he needs to ask for forgiveness?

brated. For the first time, Michael noticed the prayer of confession and the offering of God's forgiveness. He desperately wants to be in a different place in his relationships with his family and friends, and he wonders if forgiving them would help. But he is confused. Why would God want him to forgive when he feels such deep hurt, betrayal, and pain? What would it do for him, for his parents, or for anyone else?

Forgiveness, Justice, Reconciliation, and Wholeness

In the previous session, we learned that from the biblical perspective, forgiveness is a central concept in our life of faith. God's forgiveness is offered to us, and in turn that outpouring of grace compels us to forgive. Forgiveness also leads us toward justice, reconciliation, and wholeness. In this session, we will think theologically about forgiveness and its power to shape our relationships with others.

Theology invites us to consider a number of questions, both conceptually and practically: Who is God, and what is it that the Holy One intends

> What theological questions do you bring to the study of forgiveness? Create a group list of these questions, and place it where all may easily see it.

through the offering of forgiveness? How does God's forgiveness make a difference in our relationships with others or in the communities of which we are a part? Thinking theologically, we draw upon the resources of Scripture, tradition, history, and contemporary thinkers to ponder the nature of God, human beings, and community.

Three theological assertions provide the foundation for our reflections on forgiveness. The first claim rests on the belief that we are created to be in right relationship with God, self, others, the world, and all of creation. Second, individual and corporate sin and injustice keep us from experiencing the fullness and wholeness of these relationships. Third, we will return to the theological themes from the prior section and see how forgiveness invites us to move toward justice, reconciliation, and wholeness as we live into the larger realm of God.

When these assertions are integrated with biblical understandings from the last session, we can move toward greater theological clarity about what forgiveness is. Beginning with the next session, we will draw upon these biblical and theological assertions and use them to inform our understanding of the forgiveness process, how we forgive one another, what it means to forgive ourselves, and the difficulty of engaging forgiveness at the broader levels of community.

> **Three Theological Assertions**
> 1. God creates us to be in right relationship.
> 2. Relationships are broken by individual and corporate sin and injustice.
> 3. God intends justice, reconciliation, and wholeness.

Called to Be in Right Relationship

The first theological assertion is that God creates us to be in relationships. We know from the stories of Creation that human beings are related to every living creature and, in fact, to all of God's creation. These early stories remind us as well that humans are intimately connected to one another through the very breath of God. As we have seen, the stories of the Old and New Testament illustrate the multiple ways in which our relationships are based in understandings of covenant with God. Being created to be in relationship is a central theological claim of the Christian faith.

What is also clear from the biblical witness and from our theological claims over history is that God cares about the quality of our relationships with one another and with all of creation. We are not simply to participate in relationships based on what we receive from someone else; rather, we are called to live faithfully in order that the love of God is increased in the world. Ultimately, God intends

> What words or phrases would you add to the list describing relationships that reflect God's holy ways of living?

that our relationships reflect holy ways of living. Some words and phrases we associate with these kinds of relationships include: 1) love; 2) justice; 3) mutuality; 4) equal regard; 5) reciprocity; 6) mutually empathic and empowering; 7) emotionally accessible to self and to one another; 8) safe; and 9) honest. We are to love one another as God loves us. We are to care about the least of those among us. We are to be aware of how our need for power and control has a negative impact on the lives of others. We are to work toward deeper and more mutual ways of relating. The qualities of our relationships reflect the wellness of our soul.

Since we yearn for relationships that are good for us and for those around us, we might wonder why we settle for destructive and harmful relationships at times. We are sometimes confused by our hunger to love and to be loved, and we stay in relationships that are not good for us, believing that any relationship is better than none at all. This indicates how we have come to idolize and idealize relationships themselves rather than finding in them deeper and more profound ways of drawing near to God. Ultimately, relationships should not destroy us or others but free us to experience the fullness of God and to promote God's presence in the world around us.

Relationships affect not only the individuals involved in them but also others who surround those relationships as well. Even our most intimate and personal relationships are never solely about us and another person. The qualities embodied in our relationships become patterns of behavior for us, for others, and for the world. When we are angry and feel hatred, we project those feelings onto others. When we feel abused and rejected, it is difficult for us to believe that others will reach out to us. In contrast, when we feel loved and cared for, we find it easier to risk loving and caring for others. Our individual relationships have a ripple effect on everyone and everything that surrounds us. More importantly, the way we live our lives suggests something about our relationship with and understanding of God.

As we think about forgiveness, the centrality of relationships suggests at least two important things. First, it is impossible to think about forgiveness outside the context of our relationships with one another. Forgiveness is always a relational process. It is not something we do in an isolated and alienated fashion, even when the work of forgiveness is ours alone to do because the one who has harmed us or the one whom we have harmed is not available, not interested, or cannot participate in the process of forgiveness. And just as the fracture or brokenness happens in the context of relationships, so does our healing. Even when those most involved in the brokenness are not part of the healing process of forgiveness, there are others who surround us and support us in our processes. We work out our relationships in the context of our relationships with others.

Second, the work of forgiveness has an impact on how we relate to others beyond that relationship. Forgiving our family, partners, friends, or community makes a difference in the way we approach the rest of the world. Others benefit from the generosity of God's spirit in us. Desmond Tutu, now retired Anglican archbishop of Cape Town and past chairman of the Truth and Reconciliation Commission in South Africa, has wrestled with the realities of relationships that have been harmful and destructive not only to individuals but to a whole country and beyond. In talking about relationships,

> Return to the opening case study. What are the multiple relationships in Michael's life? How might forgiveness have an impact on these relationships?

Tutu refers to a word from his native tongue that is not easily translated into English, *ubuntu*. His description about what it means to refer to someone having ubuntu suggests important qualities for the work of forgiveness: "Then you are generous, you are hospitable, you are friendly and caring and compassionate. You share what you have.... A person with *ubuntu* is open and available to others, affirming of others, does not feel threatened that others are able and good."[1] Forgiveness requires this quality of which Tutu speaks. At the same time, as we engender that spirit in our relationships with others, ubuntu is passed on in the world.

The Nature of Sin

Understanding the nature of sin is directly related to how we think about forgiveness. Failures in our relationships with ourselves, with God, and with others provide the occasions to talk about and practice forgiveness. We know that sin keeps us from deepening our relationship with God and with others. Without acknowledging the reality of sin, there would be no need of a forgiveness process. Theologians throughout the ages have attempted to define precisely what we mean by the nature of sin. Terms such as *missing the mark, failure,*

> How do you understand *sin*?

original sin, trespasses, and *injustice* are only a few of the words that have come to suggest something about the nature of what it means to be humans who are created in the image of God and who break covenant with the Holy One through our sins.

> What sins seem apparent in Michael's story? Why are they "sins"?

Two significant dimensions related to sin are helpful in our consideration of forgiveness. First, when we break covenants with God, with one another, with ourselves, and with creation, we sin. Injustice, attitudes, and behaviors that harm others—actions that separate us from the love of neighbor and God—are all indications of sin. Through sin we become estranged from God, and our brokenness affects our relationships with others and with our own souls. Our failures in relationship are felt by those whom we hurt directly but also by others who experience the pain of the estrangement or who become the recipients of our displaced pain.

When we do not see ourselves and others completely and wholly, we tend to disconnect ourselves even from our very own souls. We carry distorted images of others, of our own sense of being, and even of God's love and grace. Such distortions make us more prone to blame ourselves or others for our misfortunes. Depression, despair, and hopelessness can set in. Our brokenness in relationships has a broader impact on the way we experience our relationship with the Holy One and God's creation. We become broken communities whose ability to seek peace, justice, and reconciliation is limited by our individual and collective anger, hurt, despair, and hopelessness.

> What situations of anger, hurt, or despair have limited your ability to seek peace, justice, or reconciliation?

This leads us to the second dimension of sin important for considering forgiveness. Sin is an odd combination of both individual and corporate brokenness. Our most personal fractures can never be isolated from the brokenness we experience in our communities and in the world. Likewise, the corporate nature of our lives has an impact on how we respond to individuals in our lives. Sometimes corporate sin is intentional, as in seeking revenge and hurting others because they have harmed us. Other times sin is unintentional, such as when we participate in systemic and almost invisible injustices. For example, we begin to relate to persons whose skin is a different color or to persons who do not have the financial means to provide for their children in ways that are more determined by the culture than by our understanding of God's extended love to all.

> What are some examples from our culture of corporate brokenness or sin?

This discussion of sin illuminates three aspects of forgiveness. First, forgiveness requires that we be honest about being sinful creatures, whether we are conscious or unconscious of those sins or whether the sins are individual or corporate. We are to face our souls and communities with openness and a deliberate examination of our lives. Perhaps the Wesleyan notion of asking people how it is with their souls illustrates this well. John Wesley, founder of the movement out of which emerged a number of denominations in addition to the various Methodist churches, was not simply interested in whether people felt happy or good. Wesley wanted people to be transparent and honest before God and one another. We are required to remember and not forget the sins of individuals and of the world. Forgiveness offers a way for us to remember our past and present brokenness with honesty.

Second, forgiveness suggests that while we are sinful creatures by nature, sin is not the last word. United Methodist theologian Gregory Jones suggests this when he says, "Human beings are called...to remember the past truthfully, to repair the brokenness, to heal divisions, and to reconcile and renew relationships."[2] We are called not only to be aware of our sin but also to work to change our way of being in the world. As Jones suggests, we must unlearn "the habits of sin as we seek to become holy people capable of living in communion."[3] In other words, it is not enough simply to ask forgiveness of God and one another when we are aware of and name our sins. Repentance and a change in our behavior or attitudes are central to forgiveness. Hence, sin does not have to be the final word.

Third, forgiveness assumes that God is hurt by our brokenness. Bruce Birch, academic dean and biblical scholar, once suggested to me in conversation that perhaps forgiveness is God's way of healing the soul of God from the brokenness the Holy One experiences as a result of our breaking covenant. As was evident in our examination of Scriptures, God provides ways to restore those relationships. Ultimately, forgiveness becomes one process in the larger vision of God's hope for the world. It is not that the forgiveness itself brings immediate reconciliation; rather, it is that the process of forgiveness puts in place the relational dynamics that can move us toward embodying the shalom that God intends.

God Intends Justice, Reconciliation, and Holiness

What does God intend for us in our relationships with one another, with the Holy One, with creation, and with ourselves? God intends that we live

31

in a world of shalom and holiness, marked by justice, reconciliation, and wholeness. Such a world becomes a place of wholeness for individuals and communities. Hence, we seek to restore relationships when they are damaged and covenants are broken, whether the separation is between God and humans or humans with one another. We desire this not simply

Return to the case study on pages 25–26. What does God intend for Michael, his family, and his relationships with others?

because we want to feel better but also because we believe that God intends healing and restoration of all of creation. Justice, reconciliation, and wholeness are broader aims of God's realm.

Read Micah 6:8; Isaiah 58:6-9; Luke 4:16-19. How does forgiveness connect or relate to the themes of mercy and justice in these Scriptures?

Justice is our ability to address wrongs that are systemic and broad as well as individual. For a long time in our American culture, we have depended upon the judicial system to maintain justice. What we know, however, is that the kind of justice God would have for us is difficult to achieve in the retributive nature of our court systems. Justice is not about revenge, retribution, retaliation, or paying people back for the wrongs they have done. Seeking justice recognizes that we are called to take actions that will move the world toward God's justice, not toward

Look up the word *justice* in a Bible dictionary. Note the connections with the concept of righteousness. How does your research inform your understanding of justice?

revenge and hatred. Another way to contemplate what it means to work toward justice is to think about how we restore relationships and wholeness to all involved in sin and oppression. Restoring relationships with others requires honesty, courage, and openness.

God intends for everyone to be healed, including those who have done us harm. This is sometimes a very difficult reality to accept. In the closing pages of his book *No Future Without Forgiveness,* Tutu suggests, "In the act of forgiveness we are declaring our faith in the future of a relationship and in the capacity of the wrongdoer to make a new beginning."[4] Reconciliation is a larger and more pervasive intention of God for the world. A core belief guiding the Truth and Reconciliation Commission in South Africa was the belief that God wants to restore the land, the people, and the community. Yet restoration and reconciliation happen only when we attend to the brokenness in our relationships. As Tutu suggests, "In the spirit of *ubuntu*, the central concern is the healing of breaches, the redressing of imbalances, the restoration of broken relationships, a seeking to rehabilitate both the victim and the perpetrator, who should be given the opportunity to be reintegrated into the community he has injured by his offense."[5]

Forgiveness fits into God's intentions, as the process works to restore our particular relationships in ways that embody justice, reconciliation, and wholeness. As we move through the process of forgiveness, we find ways to restore and reclaim God's intentions for the world. What this requires is honest remembering about the pain and damage that have been done to relationships in the process. As Tutu reminds us, "Forgiving and being reconciled are not about pretending that things are other than they are. . . . True reconciliation exposes the awfulness, the abuse, the pain, the degradation, the truth. It could even sometimes make things worse. It is a risky undertaking but in the end it is worthwhile, because in the end dealing with the real situation helps to bring real healing."[6]

Summary

Forgiveness is the process into which God invites us as we seek to restore our relationships with one another, with ourselves, with our communities, with the world, and ultimately with God. As we have seen, forgiveness is the gracious invitation of a God who creates us in relationship and who desires healing and wholeness for all of creation. The process of forgiveness offers us a way to deal honestly with the sins of our lives, to restore relationships that can be restored, and to find new ways of relating into the future for those relationships where restoration is not possible. Finally, forgiveness provides us with a way to move closer toward God's intention of justice, reconciliation, and wholeness, ultimately deepening our connections not simply to ourselves and others but to the very soul of God.

In the process of forgiveness, we not only work on those relationships that are most immediate to us and the places of our conscious pain, but we also create new ways of relating and living in the world. Forgiveness is offered not simply so that we may be released from our anger and pain but so that we may change the world by the way we live.

Several years ago, while I was interviewing people about issues of forgiveness, I found myself at a potter's studio outside Berea, Kentucky. Jeffrey Enge, the potter, suggested to me that clay is one of the most forgiving of materials. When I asked him what he meant, he said that the mistakes and humanness of the potter are transformed into the distinctiveness and beauty of the vessel. Forgiveness does not suggest that we wipe away any memory of our wrongdoings. Instead, through forgiveness, we find new ways to take the damage and hurt of our lives and relationships and craft them into holy vessels who promote God's vision for the world.

Closing Worship

Pray silently for a deeper awareness of how God moves in us and others as we wrestle with our failures in relationships, our corporate sins, and our need for forgiveness. Close by praying together the Lord's Prayer.

Additional Resources

Embodying Forgiveness: A Theological Analysis, by L. Gregory Jones (William B. Eerdmans Publishing Company, 1995).

An Ethic for Enemies: Forgiveness in Politics, by Donald W. Shriver, Jr. (Oxford University Press, 1998).

No Future Without Forgiveness, by Desmond Mpilo Tutu (Doubleday, 1999).

Notes

[1] From *No Future Without Forgiveness,* by Desmond Mpilo Tutu (Doubleday, 1999); page 31.

[2] From *Embodying Forgiveness: A Theological Analysis,* by L. Gregory Jones (William B. Eerdmans Publishing Company, 1995); page xii.

[3] From *Embodying Forgiveness: A Theological Analysis*; page 63.

[4] From *No Future Without Forgiveness*; page 273.

[5] From *No Future Without Forgiveness*; pages 54–55.

[6] From *No Future Without Forgiveness*; pages 270–71.

CHAPTER 3
THE PROCESS OF FORGIVENESS

Focus: Forgiveness is a process that occurs over time. While it has some predicable aspects, everyone moves through the process in different ways, at various speeds, and with a wide range of emotions.

Case Study

Elizabeth is a forty-five-year-old member of the church school class and a teacher at the local community college. She and her two children have attended the same church for many years. Her children are now in college. Elizabeth and her husband divorced several years ago, and her friends in the church walked with her through those days of grief and loss. Recently her uncle Bob died, and Elizabeth has discovered a bundle of feelings that have lived below the surface for most of her life. As a young child, Elizabeth was sexually abused by her uncle Bob. She has never talked to anyone in her family about the numerous times Uncle Bob "visited" her, nor has she told anyone during her adult life (including her ex-husband) that this is part of her history. As an adult, she decided that the abuse was something in the past, and it was something she should "forgive and forget." This strategy seems to have worked until now. As family members and friends talk about the love Uncle Bob shared with them, she finds herself feeling anger, guilt, shame, and grief. The events of the past live within her on a daily basis. She would like to talk about the impact of these experiences on her life over the years, but Elizabeth is aware that if she begins to tell the truth about the past, she will have to deal with her mother's guilt over not seeing what was going on, the disappointment of other family members in her or Uncle Bob, perhaps her ex-husband's wish that she had told him sooner, and the anger of those who think these things are better left unsaid. She wonders now how to forgive.

> Read the case study together and begin to respond to four questions: 1) Who needs to be forgiven? 2) For what do persons in this case need to be forgiven? 3) Who needs to offer the forgiveness? 4) What might the process of forgiveness look like for Elizabeth, her family, her ex-husband, her church, or her friends?

Complex Questions About Forgiveness

The story of Elizabeth raises a number of complex questions about forgiveness: What does it mean to forgive someone for harmful actions that occurred in the distant past? Does forgiveness always require the participation of the other? How do you "do" forgiveness when the one who harmed you is no longer living, does not want to participate in the process, or refuses to acknowledge any wrongdoing? What are the benefits of forgiveness—for the one who has been harmed, for the perpetrator of the harmful act, or for others related to these individuals? These questions are complex and require us to struggle with what forgiveness is and how we forgive within our individual relationships, within our families, and

> In addition to those mentioned, what questions do you have about forgiveness?

36

within the communities of which we are a part. As we noted in the last chapter, forgiveness is an offering of God that invites us to move toward deeper, more faithful ways of relating to God, self, and others as we work through those times when we disappoint one another, hurt one another (intentionally or unintentionally), or participate in forms of injustice (knowingly or unconsciously).

The Forgiveness Process

Forgiveness is first and foremost a process, not an event. The process of forgiveness occurs over time and involves a series of movements and changes in our relationships with self, God, and others. These movements are not stepping stones or stages through which we progress in a linear fashion; instead, the process of forgiveness is embodied in the ways we relate to one another at multiple levels. Much like different movements of the same symphony, each phase of the forgiveness process is distinct and yet interrelated to the others. Ultimately, forgiveness moves us toward renewed and deepened relationships not only with the ones who have harmed us but also with the broader community.

During the forgiveness process, the dynamics of our relationships may change. These transitions are sometimes painful, sometimes healing, and sometimes incredibly difficult and disturbing. The movements of the process are neither routine nor regular, even while there are some predictable aspects. The process does not occur in the same way for any two people; nor is it a process that one

> Movements in the forgiveness process:
> • A hurt is inflicted or an injustice experienced.
> • The hurt is recognized.
> • Feelings arise as a result of the inflicted pain and remain throughout the process.
> • A mutual recognition of wrongs done and harm caused changes relationships.
> • Mutual movements toward repentance, change, and / or restitution take place.
> • Resulting changes occur in the dynamics of multiple relationships.
> • Perhaps there are movements toward reconciliation.

can move through in planned, resolute, or willful ways. While intentional attitudes might be helpful, more often forgiveness is a process that surprises us, catches us off guard, or stirs our feelings and emotions in unforeseen ways.

Naming the Hurt

The process of forgiveness is intimately connected with the episode that initially caused hurt, pain, or injury to individuals or to relationships. Hence, the very first movement in the forgiveness process arises when harm is inflicted or an injustice occurs. This creates the occasion—at some point—to contemplate and enter the forgiveness process. At times it is readily apparent to those involved and to others who witness an event that something has gone wrong. For instance, when someone is involved in a traffic accident where others are killed, those who witness the incident either personally or through its retelling in the daily news know that something tragic has happened and that there will be feelings of anger, grief, guilt, and perhaps forgiveness.

At other times, injury and hurt may occur, and those involved may not even be aware of any feelings of being harmed or wronged. This may be true because there are some experiences that cause so much pain that the totality of their impact on our psyches and spirits is too much to bear all at once. Or, we may not be cognizant that something has hurt us until later in our lives when we have the capacity to understand the deeper meanings of events. The latter is often the case with children, who may be aware that they feel the pain and hurt of harm to their bodies as a result of episodes of physical or sexual violence but are less likely to be conscious of the deeper psychic and spiritual harm that the violence has caused in their lives until much later.

At some point in the process, someone recognizes that harm has occurred or that an injustice has been inflicted. Sometimes the person who has been harmed comes to the realization that something painful has happened to them. At other times, the injustice is named by those around the individual. For example, the abused child may not recognize that harm has occurred through physical or sexual abuse. However, the adults in this child's life may recognize that inappropriate sexual activity has occurred and name the trauma as abusive, recognizing that the child will carry not only physical scars but emotional and spiritual scars from the experience.

In order for the forgiveness process to move forward, it is important that those involved be as clear as possible about the particular sins, actions, behaviors, or attitudes for which they seek forgiveness for themselves or from others. Talking about forgiveness in a generalized manner does not often address our deeper need to name the particularity of harm that has been done to us. At some point in the forgiveness process, it is important to name the sins and wrongdoings that have been done or the acts that have caused harm with a sense of specificity and particularity.

Answering the questions of who needs to be forgiven, for what, and by whom can lead to a deeper awareness of feelings of anger, pain, guilt, or remorse that are being carried not only by ourselves but also by others. More often than we would like, the places of hurt in our lives are complicated by the fact that there is neither a single cause nor a single forgiveness that needs to happen. Instead, our forgiveness processes are complicated by the fact that they are multifaceted and complex.

Form teams of two or three. Spend some time naming the transgressions or sins in the story of Elizabeth. Remember that there are multiple layers and many players in the scenario. Some questions to consider are: 1) Is the only sin with which Elizabeth struggles that of her uncle's abuse of her, or could there be other places of pain and harm that Elizabeth feels in the depths of her soul? 2) How might she understand the fact that other adults around her did not "see" what she was experiencing or going through? 3) Does she carry anger at herself for not "telling someone" when she was a child? 4) Even though she intellectually knows that she was a child and had no control over the situation, what does she do with her feelings of guilt about her "participation" in the process? 5) What about the other adults who did not notice that something was wrong? 6) Could there be places of accountability in the generations before Uncle Bob?

This task of naming the hurt and the harm can serve ultimately as a structure of accountability for all those who have participated in the wrongdoing, whether as major participants or as bystanders. Looking beyond the actual participants in a situation to contemplate whether the broader systems of culture and church carry some responsibility in some cases is a significant movement in the process. The church has not always been a strong, vocal proponent of truth-telling or of speaking out against violence and abuse. For many years, our theology and tradition perpetuated images of God and humans that encouraged us to remain silent, be submissive, or even give our lives for others in ways that do not lead to wholeness. Often we actively discourage people from speaking openly and honestly about the harm that has been done to them or that they have caused, wishing for easier ways of dealing with issues like abuse and violence. Because of this, the church and those who have participated in its

In what ways has the church given implicit permission for violence in our culture or in our world? Why do we not speak out more often against abuse to children and women or against the incessant violence that we see around us? Read the story of Tamar in 2 Samuel 13:7-14. How often have you heard this text used in a sermon or as an illustration of the harm of violence? Are there other biblical stories that we have not acknowledged as part of our heritage and for which we ought to offer new interpretations and new readings?

life over time carry some responsibility for the perpetuation of abuse and violence in our culture. In some way, the church needs to ask forgiveness for its complacency in the past. As a church that exists in the culture, we are all accountable to the victims of violence in this sense, even though we have not all actively participated in the perpetration of violence.

Throughout the process, feelings will arise in the individuals and communities involved. These emotions will vary in intensity and tone as individuals and relationships struggle with such emotions as hurt, pain, anger, fear, revenge, sadness, or feelings of abandonment. Feelings are not only normal and natural, but they are also gifts from God that help us discern what is most important to attend to at any moment in time or where the deepest hurt and pain reside. In fact, these feelings are important to forgiveness, for they provide the energy and impetus to continue on in the process. Feelings are God's way of reminding us that there are important relationships at stake in our movements through forgiveness—relationships with self, others, and with God. Feelings operate as markers on the journey, and they are to be honored, even when they are intense and painful.

Mutuality in the Forgiveness Process

In the best of all possible situations, mutuality between persons enhances the forgiveness process, as those involved seek deeper and stronger relationships with one another. The hope is that the one who has done harm or perpetrated the offense will seek forgiveness, just as the one who has been harmed discovers a desire or need to forgive. Unfortunately, this sense of mutual investment is not always present. In these cases, the one who has done harm is often not able or willing to acknowledge that she or he is in the wrong.

40

When forgiveness is not a mutual process of recognizing the hurt, naming it, and acknowledging the consequences, those who are harmed are left to work through the process as much as possible on their own or with the help and support of pastors, friends, church school classes, or pastoral counselors. When mutual forgiveness is not possible, releasing the other from the process and continuing to do what work is possible by ourselves and with God frees us to embrace the abundant life and frees us from a web of anger and revenge. The process may stall at this point, and we may never be able to move toward more mutual ways of relating to another with a sense of reconciliation or peace. In fact, there are times when this is the most faithful way of responding to a situation. When this happens, it does not mean that we cannot come to terms with and feel at peace with ourselves and with God; rather, it suggests that there are times when the process will be incomplete.

> When have you felt "stalled" in the forgiveness process?

If the one who inflicted harm is able and willing to participate in the process, the forgiveness process takes a different shape. When there is mutual investment in the relationship, there is a stronger chance that the working out of forgiveness may lead toward deeper and healthier ways of relating. Just as true, however, is the reality that such mutuality does not come with guarantees that the processes will be painless or smooth. As we know, people experience the same event but see it from incredibly different perspectives, and this complicates the process. It may take a long time for the mutual naming of the injury and the harm to occur simply because persons bring their own perspectives, histories, and complexities to the forgiveness process. In these cases, it is often true that the movement of naming the hurt or the pain takes longer as people negotiate the issues of what happened and how the hurt occurred. The back-and-forth nature of this part of the forgiveness process requires incredible steadfastness with one another as we try to hear from the other how our actions have hurt that person and receive at the same time new information from the person about how she or he has been hurt in the process. We will not always like what we hear. Sometimes we turn to blame rather than asking for clarity about perceptions. But just as every word spoken does not contain the whole truth, speaking honestly and forthrightly does help us arrive at broader perspectives about the multiple truths with which we all live.

Confession, repentance, change, and restitution incorporate another series of movements in the forgiveness process. In this process of nam-

41

ing one's own sin and of laying claim to the harm that has been experienced by the other, there is a genuine desire to repent and change behavior. Sometimes this repentance involves ways of making restitution, or paying for damages that have been incurred in the process. If the relationship is built on a foundation of mutuality and trust, there might also be a sense that the one who has been hurt might find that there are things for which he or she would seek forgiveness. Perhaps the one who has been hurt needs forgiveness for holding on to the hurt, anger, or revenge, or perhaps he or she needs forgiveness for being unwilling to claim his or her own agency in moving toward healing.

Ultimately, the forgiveness process moves us toward new ways of relating with those who have hurt us, with the ones whom we have harmed, and with others with whom we have relationships. In part, the gift of forgiveness is that it invites us toward new ways of being with and relating to others. The way we move through the forgiveness process has a deep effect on the way in which we relate to others and, ultimately, to the God who forgives.

Forgiveness and Reconciliation

In some situations, reconciliation and peacefulness in the relationship mark a transition from the forgiveness process. One of the dangers in the forgiveness process is that we are so very anxious to reconcile with one another that we make reconciliation our goal. Additionally, we are uneasy with the messy feelings that arise in the process and wish that the discomfort of the process—and, indeed, the process itself—would go away. When this happens, the process is often short-circuited, resulting in lingering feelings of hurt and pain that will come to visit us in some other way when we least expect it. Reconciliation is not the goal of the forgiveness process; however, it may be an important byproduct of the process. What we hope for in forgiveness is not only that our relationships with others will be healthier but that we will also have a stronger relationship with God. While some hurts are never worked through completely during our lives on earth, we can hope that some of the significant pains of our lives will find healing and wholeness through the grace-filled movements of forgiveness. There are times that we need to hand the process over to God, trusting in God's ability to continue the work of forgiveness. We believe in a God who transcends and who has time beyond us.

Released From the Pain

In working through the forgiveness process, we are released from holding on to the pain, anger, and resentment that occur when we experience hurt or injustice. Although those who surround us may not be aware of the depths of our pain and hurt, the prayers of others become significant, as they invite us into the awareness of God's gift to us through the community that holds us. Friends, church school members, pastors, and others become witnesses and bystanders to the process of forgiveness as they see changes in our lives and the way we relate to ourselves, to our histories, and to other people. In many ways, this is the ultimate gift of forgiveness, as it has an impact not only on our individual lives and relationships but also on the way we live our lives beyond these relationships.

> Return to the case study of Elizabeth. What is the goal of forgiveness for Elizabeth, for her family, and for her relationships with others and with God? Since Uncle Bob can no longer participate in the process, can forgiveness ever be complete? Is it enough for Elizabeth to come to some peace and understanding about what has happened to her? How might her faith, her church, her pastor, and others play a roll in the forgiveness process with her? What can we pray for with Elizabeth?

Conclusion

What we hope for in the process of forgiveness is that the honesty of naming our hurts, pains, sins, and injustices will lead us not only to a deeper awareness of God's grace but will also lead us to embrace the fullness and abundance of our relationships with one another and with ourselves. The forgiveness process requires careful and honest work by those involved, lest more harm and hurt be added to already painful relationships. The process might take a matter of minutes when the harm or hurt has been experienced in a cursory or simple fashion, such as when someone accidentally bumps into you while standing in line. However, the deeper hurts and pains of our lives can take many days, seasons, months, or years to process. Even after decades, there are times when the forgiveness work is still in process and is not complete.

Closing Worship

Sing or read together the hymn "Forgive Our Sins as We Forgive" or another favorite hymn about forgiveness. Close with the Lord's Prayer.

Additional Resources

Helping People Forgive, by David W. Augsburger (Westminster / John Knox Press, 1996).

Exploring Forgiveness, edited by Robert D. Enright and Joanna North (University of Wisconsin Press, 1998).

Forgiveness Is a Choice: A Step-by-Step Process for Resolving Anger and Restoring Hope, by Robert D. Enright (American Psychological Association, 2001).

The Art of Forgiving: When You Need to Forgive and Don't Know How, by Lewis B. Smedes (Ballantine Books, 1997).

CHAPTER 4
THE RELATIONAL WORK
OF FORGIVING OTHERS

Focus: Invitations to practice the art of forgiveness occur daily in our relationships with family members, friends, and colleagues. This chapter will explore attitudes, belief systems, and ways of relating that can assist us in moving through the process with others. It will show how identifying barriers in the process with others can help us stay on track.

Gathering

Read Genesis 50:15-21 and recall the story of Joseph and his brothers. What did it mean for Joseph to forgive his brothers? What did it mean for the brothers to forgive Joseph? What helped them in this process? What stood in their way? Pray for those in relationships who struggle daily to forgive one another.

Christianity Teaches Forgiveness

Forgiveness is a central teaching of Christian faith. Consider what traditional Christian interpretations or understandings of forgiveness might mean in the situations described below.

Isabel and Pablo have been married for almost twenty-five years. Their youngest child is about to leave home to enter college. Isabel and Pablo have spent most of their financial and emotional resources on assisting their children, and they have not attended nearly as well to their own relationship. Resentment has built over the years, with Isabel wishing that Pablo would pay more attention to their children and to her instead of to his career and Pablo longing to move into the upper management of the organization for which he works. They have come to an impasse recently because Pablo has been offered a position that would require him to travel more and be away from home. Isabel was looking forward to the children moving out of the house and to spending more time with Pablo. The decision-making has resulted in hurt and pain, as each is having a hard time hearing and responding to the other. Recently Isabel suggested to Pablo that they seek a separation.

Jason is thirty-five years old, the only son of a wealthy and prosperous family whose business is one of the strongest in the community. Jason's father retired from the business two years ago, and Jason took over the daily operations. He has always been an incredibly responsible son. Recently Jason has felt more dissatisfied in his work and is contemplating leaving the family business. He is aware of the tremendous pain this would bring to his family and the feelings of anger, hurt, and disappointment from his father and mother in particular. Jason feels boxed in and begins to self-medicate through alcohol. His parents are considering options for intervention.

> Divide into four teams. Each team should read and respond to one of the case studies. Who needs to be forgiven in these cases? For what do they need forgiveness? Who needs to offer forgiveness? How might the process of forgiveness be moved along in each case? What might get in the way of the forgiveness process? Report the highlights of your team discussion to the entire group.

Nikki and Dominique work together and have become like sisters to one another. Recently Nikki disclosed a confidence to Dominique and asked her not to share it with anyone else. Dominique, however, felt that Nikki's secret could cause her and others significant harm. She went to another mutual friend and talked about what to do. The friend later approached Nikki, letting her know that she knew about the situation in her life. Nikki felt betrayed, angered, and humiliated by Dominique's disclosure to their friend, vowing never to speak to either one of them again.

Eileen ended up in the emergency room of the hospital with a broken rib caused when her partner, Richard, hit her in a fit of rage. Richard had returned home after work and found the children angry and upset. In turn, Richard grew angry and took it out on Eileen, because he assumes that it is Eileen's responsibility to take care of things at home while he is at work. This is not the first time physical abuse has occurred in their relationship. Richard never hits the children and is quick to feel remorse and ask for forgiveness. Eileen understands that Christians forgive one another and that marriage is for life. Richard believes he is the head of the household and responsible for keeping things in order.

Relational Forgiveness

Opportunities to practice the art of forgiveness arise when our relationships have been fractured or when we feel hurt and pain in response to the actions, behaviors, or oppressions of individuals or communities around us. Sometimes the injury is a result of intentional harm inflicted by someone close to us. At other times, the hurt arises through actions that are not necessarily intended to inflict pain but that hurt us nonetheless. At still other times, the wound is an unintentional byproduct of some larger systemic injustice such as racism or classism. No matter what the circumstances, the fracturing of relationships and the damage that ensues create opportunities to practice the art of forgiveness.

As we work through forgiveness, three relational aspects are present. First, it is important to remember that forgiveness is always a process that requires and depends upon our being related to others. Relationships that are healthy and holy—not necessarily perfect—can be life-giving. But even in the most life-giving of relationships, we hurt one another unintentionally. For whatever reasons, we speak painful words or participate in activities that hurt those whom we love. The inevitability of experiencing some kind of pain in our relationships is one of those deep theological issues related to the reality of both being created as relational beings and of being sinful creatures. The forgiveness process becomes one of the means to deepen and strengthen good relationships. At the same time, the process helps us assess those relationships that might always be harmful to us in the future.

The relational context of forgiveness is by far one of the most complex realities of the forgiveness process itself. Hurt and pain do not occur in a vacuum, in isolation, or as a result of anything other than our relatedness to others. On the one hand, we like to believe that we can practice forgiveness without the assistance of the one who has harmed us, that the

Find a partner and talk about the following questions: 1) When have you felt that the practice of forgiveness was yours to do and that you could negotiate the pain and hurt on your own? 2) What were the circumstances? 3) Were you successful? Why or why not? 4) How were the people around you affected by your working on the forgiveness process on your own?

work of forgiveness is ours to do, and that we can negotiate the hurt and pain on our own (or perhaps with the assistance of a good friend, a therapist, or a pastor). Indeed, there are many aspects of the process that we must journey through on our own, in spite of the presence or absence of others in the process. At times this independence suggests to us that the forgiveness process is something we do only to make us feel better, not necessarily something we do to improve or enhance our relationships. The reality is that forgiveness is not simply for the sake of our own well-being or feeling good. The core purpose of forgiveness is to enhance, deepen, and strengthen the goodness of our relationships with ourselves, with others, with the world, and with God.

On the other hand, we are often so eager to repair relationships that are important to us that we tend to ignore or deny some of the destructive qualities of harmful interactions that cause us pain. The temptation to move too quickly toward reconciliation sometimes means that we sacrifice the potential value that the forgiveness process holds for the relationship itself or for the well-being of our own lives. When forgiveness is either practiced as an isolated activity only for personal benefit or well-being, or when it becomes a means to retain relationships in spite of negative and harmful consequences, the process itself is distorted. A relationship is to be valued but not to the point that the qualities leading to wholeness for all are no longer present.

What are some examples of relationships that demonstrate negative or harmful consequences?

A second relational aspect of forgiveness is that it allows us the time and intentional space to assess the quality of our relationships with others and to note their strengths and limitations. Some of our relationships are so essential and strong that the process of forgiveness, while painful, serves to deepen and build up the positive aspects. Other relationships—in fact, probably most of our relationships—are more mixed. We recognize the limitations of good friendships, yet we desire loving and caring people around us who can sit with us in our pain and celebrate with us in our joys. Finally, there are some relationships that are harmful to us, to our families, or to the general community around us, and the forgiveness process allows us to recognize these, grieve them, and move away from them.

The level of mutual depth and commitment within a particular relationship provides clues about how the forgiveness process might proceed. The relational quality of the process can be one of the most redemptive, and it can

> Find a partner. Talk together about examples of essential and strong relationships, some examples of acquaintances or friendships that are not as essential but that could be important to you, and some examples of relationships that are harmful in some way. How do you see the forgiveness process at work in each of these illustrations?

also be one of the most dangerous and difficult aspects of forgiveness. It is important to come to terms with the reality that just because forgiveness is a relational process, this does not mean that we should place ourselves in harm's way or be vulnerable in ways that lead to emotional, spiritual, or physical harm. God does not call us to sacrifice our lives in this way for the sake of holding on to a relationship. To recognize that relationship is at the core of the forgiveness process means that we distinguish "our" work from the work of the "other." We must also assess the potential for repairing the relationship. Forgiveness requires careful attention to the dynamics of

> How do you move through the process of forgiveness if those who are involved in the relational context cannot or will not participate? Is forgiveness enough if it only helps the individual who has been hurt? How does one forgive without being set up to feel hurt and pain all over again by either offering forgiveness too quickly or capitulating to the wishes and desires of others in ways that are not healthy?

the relationship and the capacity of those in our relationships to work the process. What needs to remain central to the process is taking an intentional time to assess the strengths, vulnerabilities, and capacity of a relationship to move toward embodying the wholeness articulated in the gospel. Not every relationship can or should be retained. Relationships that are not created out of love, justice, and mutuality are often relationships that can never be fully whole. In these latter cases, forgiveness is something we must work on in ways that allow us to let go of and to grieve those relationships that are destructive to us or to those whom we love.

Third, forgiveness operates in our relational lives as a structure of accountability.[1] The process becomes one way to nurture those relationships that are most important to us, allowing us to address our pains honestly and to work toward restoring wholeness in these relationships. As a structure of accountability, the forgiveness process provides a means for naming even the simplest ways that we hurt one another. The process allows us to be honest about our relationships and, ultimately, provides us with opportunities to act in ways that embody love and care.

As we negotiate the differences and the pains present even in the best relationships, we build upon the strength, health, and wholeness of those relationships. Even in the best processes, injury and pain occur. The truth is that we almost always injure those whom we love as we seek to be heard, to get our needs met, and to listen carefully. Yet, because forgiveness allows us both to name our hurt and to have that pain acknowledged, forgiveness operates as a structure of accountability that further strengthens our relationships. The process allows us to embrace mutual ways of relating that honor one another and that seek the best for one another's lives. In this way, the forgiveness process allows us to account for the normal hurts and pains of even very healthy and whole relationships.

Supports for the Process of Forgiving Others
- Mutuality
- Honesty
- Ability to listen deeply and fully
- Patience and steadfastness
- Praying God's best intentions for the other

What Supports the Process of Forgiving Others?

At least five qualities assist individuals, families, and communities as they move through the forgiveness process. First, mutuality is essential to the process, particularly if we want to retain relationships with one another beyond the hurt. To suggest that relationships are mutual implies that there is give-and-take between people. Power is shared in ways that benefit everyone involved in the relationship, and partners work toward seeing that the best interests of others are served as much as our own. Mutuality suggests that there is equity in the relationships and that persons do not hold one another hostage emotionally or spiritually.

50

Through our mutual acknowledgment with others, we recognize that there are ways in which we share responsibility for the pain and hurt of a relationship, even though we may not be the one who initially caused the harm. Such mutuality also suggests that we are partners, in some sense, as we work through the process. Just as I take one move in the process, the one whom I have hurt takes another. Unfortunately the steps do not always match, and there are times that reinjury or further hurt occurs. Misunderstandings and misinterpretations can lead to ongoing hurt. Yet, the power of forgiveness is that it refuses to give up on good and healthy relationships.

The stronger the mutual investment between individuals, the better chance the forgiveness process has of resulting in deeper and more meaningful relationships. In relationships marked by mutuality, we have the other person's best interest at heart as well as our own as we move through the process. Again, there are times when such mutuality is not present in a relationship—when the other is less invested or less interested in wholeness. At such times, it is important to walk away and to seek help from others whom you trust or from a trained professional. Recognizing the importance of relationships does not minimize the need for self-care as we live in and through them.

> How has mutuality been involved in situations where you have worked at the process of forgiving others?

Second, the capacity for honesty is important in the forgiveness process. Our ability to be honest, without being cruel to one another, enhances the possibility of having a forgiveness process that builds one another up rather than destroying the self-esteem of one another. Speaking and hearing the truth from one another requires vulnerability and generosity as we openly share our thoughts, experiences, perceptions, and concerns. Honesty does not mean that we say the first thing that moves across our mind in the heat of a moment; rather, honesty is "speaking the truth in love." As such, it requires us to state clearly and carefully our own perspective without intentionally trying to hurt the other. At times our honesty will compel us

> How has honesty been involved in situations where you have worked at the process of forgiving others? Was honesty difficult for you? Why? In what ways?

to share painful feelings or realizations about ourselves or those whom we love. At other times, honesty requires us to be clear about the negative aspects of a relationship and their effect on our lives or on the lives of those around us. Such truthfulness requires us to be empowered to walk away from relationships are not healthy for us, for our family, or for others. Honesty with ourselves, with one another, and with God can deepen relationships at all levels, leading us to greater abundance in our living. Truth—spoken with love and care—becomes a healing dynamic in good relationships.

Third, listening deeply and fully is one of the more difficult but essential elements to the forgiveness process. Forgiveness requires an ability to listen and take in new information, even if it does not match our own experience or perception. This posture of deep listening is known as empathy, or the ability to suspend "one's own frame of reference in order to enter the perceptual and emotional world of the other."[2] As opposed to a stance of sympathy (feeling on behalf of the other or feeling so deeply that another's pain becomes our own pain), empathy creates a caring distance so that we can experience our own pain and at the same time attempt to understand more fully the hurt that our friend, partner, or colleague is experiencing.

Empathy is the ability to try to understand as deeply as possible the perspective of the other without being judgmental about our feelings or perceptions or the experiences and reports of others. In empathy, we acknowledge the suffering of the one whom we hurt as well as the pain of the one who has hurt us. Listening carefully suspends our judgmentalism long enough so that we can gain greater insight about ourselves and about others. Making the effort to listen fully so that we can begin to imagine what it is like for the other person to be in her or his particular place is essential to the process. This kind of deep listening requires humility, as we come to know that even our best intentions sometimes hurt others. Additionally, we sometimes discover how very wrong we have been in our perceptions of others or ourselves.

Recall times when you have felt that someone listened deeply to you. What was it like? What current situations or relationships would benefit by your offering of deep listening and empathy?

Empathy does not dismiss the pain or suspend accountability; rather, it invites us to become more aware of all of the dynamics and choices that go into any one event. The forgiveness process provides for us the emotional and spiritual space we need as we try to clarify to ourselves and to one another precisely what hurts, why it feels so painful, and what we hope for in moving through forgiveness. Realizing how our actions hurt others or becoming aware of the depth of our own pain assists us in changing and refining our perspective on a particular situation. Discernment requires that we listen deeply to ourselves and to others. We then move through the forgiveness process ready and able to restate our positions more clearly and to demonstrate our own ability to change our minds. Such careful and deep listening is a gift and a skill that can be practiced over and over again in our relationships with others.

Fourth, forgiveness requires patience and steadfastness as we allow God to work in us and in others over time. When we are too anxious to return to a feeling of homeostasis or stability in our relationships with others, we may not take the time necessary to name and change the dynamics that caused damage to the relationship in the first place. Trying to force the process to move too quickly or being impatient with one another about the way in which we engage the process will ultimately result in a distorted process. It is impossible to control the process or to make sure that others move through it in ways that we think they should.

> What situations might impede or block the call to be gracious and generous with our forgiveness?

Likewise, when we are more eager to return things to normal than we are to discern what has gone wrong and what needs to change in order not to repeat the mistakes of the past, we tend to push the process too quickly. Such swiftness does not allow for the appropriate experiences of confession, repentance, and change. Forgiveness is a process that deserves and requires time. In relationships that share a mutual sense of commitment to one another's well-being, time becomes a gift, as we sit with our uncomfortable feelings and the pain of the process itself in order to arrive at more redemptive and just ways of relating to one another.

> What do you see as challenges to the patience required of the forgiveness process? What are some ways to encourage patience in yourself as you are involved in the forgiveness process?

Fifth, praying God's best intentions for the one who has harmed us is sometimes a difficult but important part of the process. Even when we do not feel like forgiving someone, we can internally move closer to God and to the embodiment of God's way of relating to us if we practice faithful prayer for others. Like the psalmist who, at the end of the lament, is opened to hope by remembering God's past promises and deliverances, so praying God's best intentions on those who have done harm to us opens us to the possibility of the inbreaking of the Spirit in new and wondrous ways. We base our prayers not on our own human willpower or on our own sense of justice and rightness; rather, we offer intercessory prayers that allow God to invest in the wholeness of the other as much as we ask God to have an impact on our own well-being.

> Reflect prayerfully now on praying for those you need to forgive. What would be your prayer for them?

What Hinders the Process of Forgiving Others?

While there are many dynamics that impair our movement through the forgiveness process, there are three that seem most damaging. First, reverting to blaming others or feeling shame in ourselves hinders the process. When we believe that hurt and pain are one-dimensional or that there is always a clear victim and a clear perpetrator of offense, we ignore the reality that we are all participants in relational processes, both in their redemptive hope and in their sinful realities. When we fall into the trap of believing that hurt and pain are caused by one single factor or one individual, we miss the complexity of God's world and reduce it to our singleness of mind or to a simplicity that is rarely present. In many ways, what is required in the forgiveness process is a generosity of spirit that recognizes that blaming others or reverting to shame results only in a cyclical process that moves us toward greater damage and despair rather than genuine hope.

> **Hindrances to the Process of Forgiving Others**
> • Reverting to cycles of blame and shame
> • Inability to name or claim feelings
> • Lack of community

Second, those who have a hard time recognizing, dealing with, or working through emotions and feelings will have a more difficult time participating in the forgiveness process. Required throughout the process is a willingness not only to recognize our feelings and to sit with them but also to come to believe that they can guide and deepen our relationships with one another and with God. This is particularly true of feelings such as anger, hurt, and rage. Our anger can provide insight about how we have experienced hurt or where we sense the deepest injustice or damage to be found. The problem with anger is not that we have these feelings but that we often tend to deny anger's presence, or we hold on to feelings of hurt and pain in ways that become comfortable. Anger should not be denied, nor should it be nurtured into actions of revenge, hate, or "getting even." It is true that the forgiveness process can lead to deeper feelings of hurt and anger as we stumble through the process. However, if we listen to the anger and let it speak its truth to us, we can follow its path as we discern what needs to change in order for our relationships to be more reflective of the qualities of love and care that we most desire. Anger can be understood to be one of the gifts of a God who cares enough to provide us with feelings that assist us in our journey.

> Read Genesis 3:8-13. How does this Scripture illustrate blaming? What situations are you aware of in which blaming has impeded the forgiveness process?

> Read again the case study about Isabel and Pablo. How has denial of anger been involved in their marriage? What might help them enter into a process of forgiveness?

Finally, the absence of community along with the lack of the spiritual, emotional, and physical resources it provides can impede the forgiveness process. We need others around us who can support us in the midst of our fears, angers, and struggles. In particular, we need people who are willing to pray with us and for us and people who believe in the power of God's grace and forgiveness. When no one seems to be listening or caring or when we feel alone in our journey, the community of faith can become the embodied presence of God. Additionally, the community around us can assist us in discerning when relationships can be changed or strengthened and when they need to be let go of in some sense.

> Find a partner. Talk together about how family, church, or friends have supported you during difficult times. How might they support you as you seek to enter the process of forgiving someone in your life?

As we have recognized above, just because forgiveness is a relational process, we should never think that God wants us to put ourselves in danger emotionally, spiritually, or physically. Appropriate vulnerability is required in order to gain self-awareness and to deepen our relationships with others. This does not mean that we ought to be overly vulnerable to the harm that others might bring to us or that we should depend on the community to do our work for us. Instead, community provides us with companions in our journey of forgiveness and faith.

Conclusion

Forgiveness is not a solitary process or a single movement that we control on our own; instead, the process involves those to whom we are related. There are gifts and graces that can assist us on the journey of forgiveness, just as there are impediments to the process. Praying with and for another in our human attempts to work the forgiveness process can lead to healthier and holier relationships with one another and with God.

Closing Worship

Return to one of the cases from the beginning, and think about what it would mean for your church school class or community of faith to be present with these persons as they move through the forgiveness process. What would you pray for the individuals and the relationships in the case? How can you register your support while at the same time holding one another accountable for the wrongs and the harms that have occurred?

Sing or read aloud together the hymn "Help Us Accept Each Other." Pray silently for all persons in relationships who struggle to discern how to move through the forgiveness process without setting themselves up for further harm. Close by praying aloud the Lord's Prayer.

Additional Resources

Caring Enough to Confront: How to Understand and Express Your Deepest Feelings Toward Others, by David W. Augsburger (Regal Books, 1980).

The Angry Christian: A Theology for Care and Counseling, by Andrew D. Lester (Westminster/John Knox Press, 2003).

The Gift of Anger: A Call to Faithful Action, by Carroll Saussy (Westminster/John Knox Press, 1995).

Listening and Caring Skills: A Guide for Groups and Leaders, by John Savage (Abingdon Press, 1996).

Notes

[1] From "Communal Dimensions of Forgiveness: Learning From the Life and Death of Matthew Shepard," by Joretta L. Marshall, in *Journal of Pastoral Theology,* Vol. 9, 1999; pages 49–62.

[2] From "Empathy," by D. E. Massey, in *Dictionary of Pastoral Care and Counseling,* edited by Rodney J. Hunter (Abingdon Press, 1990); page 354.

CHAPTER 5
FORGIVING SELF

Focus: Forgiveness of self is difficult, but it is the appropriate response when we experience guilt from our actions, behaviors, or attitudes. It is sometimes a long and slow process, often complicated by the presence of shame and self-doubt. Often we must first work through shame in order to move toward forgiving ourselves. This session will help us to find ways to challenge the shame that binds us and to rely on the foundations of God's grace in order that we might more fully engage in relationships with others and with God.

Gathering
  Greet one another. Pray together the following prayer: "God of hope and new life, be with us today as we explore ways to forgive ourselves as you forgive us. In Christ we pray. Amen."

Case Study

Jessica is a 44-year-old woman who has always had a difficult time with her emotional life. She has been divorced for seven years, and she lives alone. Her parents are no longer living, and she has little community around her. Sharon, her only sister, lives in another state at quite some distance. Recently, Jessica was so depressed that she contemplated suicide. At the urging of her pastor, she scheduled an appointment with a counselor. After several weeks and a referral to a psychiatrist, it was determined that Jessica suffered from long-term depression. She tried the medication that was prescribed but then decided that the side effects were too strong and that she was losing her effectiveness at work. She quit taking the medication and discovered that she felt worse than she did before. Eventually, her counselor convinced

> Read the story of Jessica. Who needs to be forgiven? For what? By whom? Reflect on the role of the church in the lives of those who struggle daily with mental health. Pray for their families and for the churches that surround and support them.

her to try the medication once again. Jessica is angry not only at the medication and its effects on her life but also at herself for being depressed. She feels that she has not dealt well with her whole life and that there doesn't seem to be much hope of changing her outlook in the near future.

If there is anything more difficult than forgiving others who have hurt us, it is wrestling honestly with forgiving ourselves. Stories like Jessica's sometimes hit close to home for us, our friends, or our families. Struggles with issues of mental health such as depression, schizophrenia, bipolar disorder, and addictions are particularly challenging because we feel that we are somehow to blame for the illness. We doubt ourselves and often feel ashamed that we have such infirmities. Such stories also remind us that we are frequently better equipped to offer grace to those who have harmed us in some way than we are at being gentle with our own souls. As we confront the inner nature of our lives, we are often very aware of our shortcomings and our failures. This consciousness keeps us from engaging fully in relationships with God and with others. We are fearful that others will discover who we really are and will abandon us once they really know us. We perceive that we are less than good, and we do not ultimately believe that we are created in the image of God.

When we are stuck in our self-doubt and shame, it is difficult for us to acknowledge that we are also human beings who can be touched by the grace of God, whether we deserve it or not. We push others away, fear-

> How do you think self-doubt and shame are involved in Jessica's situation?

ing that the care they offer will not be enough to counter the deep shame we feel about our very being. We hold ourselves hostage to feelings of self-hatred or self-loathing, denying God's ability to grace us. Such shame refuses to acknowledge, claim, or affirm the reality that we are both sinful creatures *and* that we are also children of God. Instead, we hold on to our brokenness and settle for less than the abundance that God offers.

Shame and Guilt

Shame is often a deep barrier from moving forward in the process of forgiving ourselves. We cannot forgive ourselves if we do not first deal with our shame. In order to address shame and forgiveness in ourselves, we must attend to three interrelated but distinct issues: 1) distinguishing shame from guilt; 2) recognizing the power of grace in confronting our shame; and 3) contemplating how to draw upon the resources of our faith in order to forgive ourselves.

Guilt has often been confused with shame. Recognizing the difference between shame and guilt is one of the first steps in addressing the work of our inner soul. Guilt is an appropriate response to those failures and shortcomings for which we can seek forgiveness. Acknowledging the reality of our sins—our conscious and unconscious actions, behaviors, and thoughts—often awakens in us responses of guilt. The human dilemma is to separate shame from guilt so that we can allow both for the presence of God's grace in confronting our shame and be open to the power of forgiveness in responding to our guilt.

Whereas guilt is associated with the naming of sins, shame is a pervasive sense of self-loathing that prevents us from revealing who we are to ourselves, to others, and ultimately to God. The distinctive feature of shame leaves us feeling "exposed, uncovered, unprotected, vulnerable."[1] Shame is an internal sense not simply that we have done things that are wrong but that we are evil and broken in ways that make us unforgivable as human beings. Such pervasive feelings of unworthiness do not allow for grace or for the ability to recognize ourselves as children of God. In this sense, shame keeps God's grace always at a distance. Shame retains a bar-

> Form two teams. Read again the section entitled "Shame and Guilt." Team one should list some actions or situations that are likely to produce feelings of guilt. Team two should list situations that are likely to produce feelings of shame. Reconvene as one large group. Compare the lists each team developed.

rier between ourselves, God, and others because at the very core of our being, we always feel as if we are unworthy of anything good.

These feelings about ourselves keep us in bondage, as we believe that what is wrong with us is not simply that we have committed sins or errors in judgment; rather, we feel deep shame and are convinced that we are less than adequate as human beings. This sense of feeling ashamed destroys any sense of the goodness of self with which God has blessed us. Addressing shame requires that we acknowledge the abundance of God's grace for us as human beings. When we confront shame, we accept our humanity, complete with all of our limitations and vulnerabilities.

Shame is a complicated internal reality that is most commonly experienced in the knowledge that we stand naked before God. Reflecting on the Creation stories, particularly as they are told in the third chapter of Genesis, we become aware of the dynamics of shame. The human creatures stood before God feeling not simply embarrassed but ashamed. They were aware of their nakedness and vulnerability. The humans were unable to fathom a God

> Read the Creation story in the third chapter of Genesis. Is this a story about shame or about guilt? How are the two connected in the story? How are they distinct?

who would know what to do with their feelings of unworthiness and self-consciousness. Their expulsion from the garden is seen as a result of actions for which they ought to experience guilt. Yet, the pervasiveness of feelings of shame in the story makes it easy to see how guilt and shame become intertwined in our reality.

Although shame can be debilitating, it is also true that healthy doses of shame protect us in some basic ways. A healthy sense of shame helps us to be aware of how others perceive us and of appropriate ways of relating to others. Healthy shame keeps us humble and aware of our powerlessness before God while, at the same time, it allows us to receive and accept grace as it is found in God and in our relationships with others. For these reasons, it is important to honor the shame that protects the most vulnerable places of our soul.

On the other hand, unhealthy shame keeps us in bondage, as our feelings of unworthiness overwhelm us and keep any expressions of grace from touching our souls. When we assume that we are not just sinful people but that we embody sin in a way that can never be redeemed, we are living out of a base of shame that holds us hostage. Unhealthy shame assumes that we are not lovable by God or by other human beings. Hence, persons who live in constant and overwhelming shame often avoid relationships altogether, or they seem to work three times as hard as is necessary to keep other people in relationships with them. When one lives in the midst of a shame that overwhelms, one cannot approach God or others with any sense of being found acceptable in their sight.

> Reflect silently upon situations in your life or in the life of someone you know that have created an unhealthy sense of shame. Take time now to pray for God's guidance and support as you name that sense of shame and open yourself to God's healing grace.

As human beings, there is nothing that we can do to counter the internal sense of shame apart from receiving the grace of God in our lives. We cannot work our way out of shame, although it is necessary to pay attention to its debilitating feelings. There may be times when it is appropriate to enter counseling or therapy because shame has become such a hindrance to living. When this happens, the therapy becomes part of our re-claiming of ourselves; it is not that we *work* our way to salvation as much as that we *become aware of the grace of God*, thus enabling us to lay claim to our place as children of God.

Grace

Distinctive in Wesleyan theology is the high value given to the gift of grace. John Wesley understood that grace—prevenient, justifying, and sanctifying—was both God's gift *for* us and God's work *in* us. Prevenient grace is present even before we know it is there. This indwelling of God's Spirit offers us the possibility for wholeness. This grace is freely given even before we ask for it, and it becomes the foundation for our ability to respond to God. Justifying grace, "the work God does for us," brings with it a new birth in the form of "the work God does *in us*."[2] We are justified by our faith and stand before God not because we are righteous but because of our faith. We seek to live holy and faithful lives marked by faith, hope, and love in response to the gift of God's grace. As a result of the prevenient grace of God, we acknowledge justification through our faith and proclaim that we are forgiven and reconciled people. Through the new birth that is offered in our sanctification, we become *forgiving and reconciling* people who practice the art of forgiveness as part of our daily Christian journey.[3]

Before we can forgive ourselves for the wrongs we have done, frequently we must wrestle with our feelings of internal shame. We often feel shame inappropriately in those arenas of our lives over which we have no control. For example, we feel shame about having a debilitating disease or an illness of the mind or spirit. We think that there is something wrong with our very being rather than understanding that we have to accept an illness or handicapping condition over which we have no control. Accepting ourselves as we are is one of the most important elements in experiencing the grace of God. At the same time, recognizing that we do have some power and control over how we respond to these realities, we examine our own lives, and we are invited into the process of forgiving ourselves. Letting go of shame and accepting accountability for our responses requires honesty and a healthy spiritual discipline.

> Return to the story of Jessica. Identify places where you suspect she is feeling shame. How might healthy shame be operative in her life? How might inappropriate or unhealthy shame be keeping her stuck? What intercessory prayer would you offer as you speak to God on Jessica's behalf?

Because of the deep connections between guilt and shame, it is important to ascertain whether what we are in need of at any point in time is a deeper acceptance and reliance on grace or whether the salve for our soul is to move through the forgiveness process. Only when we discern whether we suffer from inappropriate shame or healthy guilt can we determine if we are in need of greater acceptance of grace or genuine forgiveness of the self.

Faith, Guilt, and Forgiving Ourselves

Being honest about our sins, our failures in human relationships, and the ways in which we have participated consciously and unconsciously in systems of injustice or oppression leads us to wonder about how to forgive ourselves. Guilt is an internal signal that encourages us to stop and take account of our own lives. When we experience genuine guilt, we must move through the process of forgiveness to name our failures, repent and change our behaviors, and attempt to amend our ways.

Just as there are healthy expressions of shame, guilt can also be healthy for us, as it insists that we be honest about our shortcomings and our sins. We are often prompted to seek forgiveness and work toward restoring relationships with others and with God when feelings of guilt arise within us. Whether guilt arises from sins of omission or commission, the process gives our spiritual self the space it needs to turn inward and honestly seek the depths of our hearts and souls. In such situations, it is important to move through the forgiveness process in ways that acknowledge one's own shortcomings and allow for the grace of God and others to penetrate our beings.

As is true with unhealthy shame, some of us also carry more than our share of guilt. Such unhealthy guilt leaves us feeling overly responsible for everything that has happened to us, to our loved ones, or to the broader community. Taking on more responsibility for the sins of the world than is rightfully ours to carry is, in some ways, a sign of lack of humility. Unhealthy guilt can drive us to self-destructive behavior or to ways of relating that are damaging to others or to ourselves. A friend once encouraged me to remember what she called the three C's: "There are some things you do not *cause*, you cannot *cure*, and over which you have no *control*." Letting go of the belief that we can control all things keeps us from the excessive guilt that can literally drive us crazy.

Excessive guilt keeps us afraid that we will hurt others or get hurt in the process of relationships. As a result, we construct barriers in our relationships with others, and we are fearful about fully engaging others. If the cause of our anxiety and distress is an unhealthy amount of guilt, then it is appropriate to seek help from pastors, pastoral counselors, or other mental-health professionals.

Movements in Forgiving Ourselves

How do we move through the process once we recognize that there are genuine things for which we need to seek forgiveness from ourselves—attitudes, beliefs, behaviors, or actions—or from others? The first step is to take a self-inventory and determine whether we are trying to ask forgiveness for a wrong we have done and a sin committed (of commission or omission) *or* if what we are struggling with is actually a sense of shame. If our struggle is to counter shame, then we need to wrestle with the knowledge and gift of God's grace. This requires that we let go of the negative hold that shame has on our lives. Such an action seems as simple as accepting the gift of grace; however, it is as difficult for people caught in the bondage of shame to accept the knowledge of prevenient grace as it is for us to find our way out of a deep fog. Ultimately, acknowledging that the grace of

> What situations in your life have caused you to feel guilt even when you did not cause them, could not cure them, and had no control over them?

God has been made available to us even without our asking for it allows for a new in-breaking of grace in our lives, and we are able to look inward with less distortion.

If what we are seeking is forgiveness from ourselves for something we have done wrong, then our task is to wrestle more completely with the sins we have committed or our failures to act. An honest acknowledgement of our wrongdoings invites us into a process of repentance. Naming our sin is not something we have to do in isolation, although there are times we would prefer to work on our own. Yet, asking for feedback from those whom we have wronged or who know and love us can provide us with more accurate pictures of ourselves and our relationships. The forgiveness process is complicated at this point by the fact that not everyone sees things from the same perspective or names sin in exactly the same way. Only through the mutual process of clarifying to ourselves and with others precisely what it is that we think we need to forgive can we discern the next steps in our process.

Movements in Forgiving Ourselves
- Taking self-inventory and naming our sins
- Acknowledging our own wrongdoings and our sins
- Asking for forgiveness from ourselves or from others
- Practicing genuine repentance that leads to change of behaviors and actions
- Remaining engaged and in dialogue with others in our spiritual and emotional journeys

As we know, repentance means to turn around or to turn from something. When God invites us to repent, we are asked not only to come to new self-awarenesses but actually to change some of our behaviors, attitudes, or actions. In repentance, we turn from attitudes, expressions, or behaviors that have created harm to others or that have perpetuated systems of injustice or oppression. It is not enough simply to say that we are sorry about particular attitudes or actions; in genuine repentance, we actually attempt to create change in ourselves. This change leads us toward self-forgiveness, as we see that the way we have related is harmful not only to others but also to ourselves. This change often takes time, and there are many opportunities in the process for "failures" to occur. Yet these are transformative processes that ultimately can lead us to claim new life in significant ways.

During the repentance process in particular, it can be important to seek reflection and honest conversation with others in our lives about our shortcomings. This humbling process provides opportunities to be open and honest in ways that make us more self-aware, and in the process, such conversations can deepen and strengthen the relationships of which we are a part. In dialogue with others, we can sometimes begin to recognize behaviors and attitudes that get in our way or that create brokenness in our relationships. At the same time, the dialogue can create new understandings about our shortcomings as well as the gifts we bring to our relationships.

In order to forgive ourselves, at times we must also seek forgiveness from others. Recognizing how our attitudes or actions have hurt our own lives or the lives of those whom we love results in a desire to seek forgiveness from self and others. Even as we ask for forgiveness from those whom we have hurt, we need to be mindful that we cannot control how others engage the process of forgiveness. We can only ask for forgiveness, genuinely repent, and invite others to enter a process that we hope will be meaningful for the relationship and for each other.

> How can the movements to forgive ourselves described in this section be helpful to you? What situations in your life would benefit from your choice to enter into these movements?

Ultimately, forgiving ourselves leads us to renewed ways of relating to others beyond ourselves. Self-forgiveness should never end only at self-examination without also changing the ways we relate to ourselves, to others, and to God. The goal of forgiveness is not simply to acknowledge that we are forgiven; rather, the goal of forgiveness is to provide a means to act and be in authentic, loving, justice-seeking, grace-infused ways of relating with self and with others. These ways of relating are rooted and grounded in God's forgiveness and grace.

Seeking Professional Help

There are times in this process when we need assistance in moving toward forgiveness of ourselves. This is particularly true when persons are stuck in shame more than they are in need of self-forgiveness. Sometimes the struggle to accept grace is harder than we imagine. Often shame is something that lives with us as a result of experiences in childhood or early in our lives. Shame can take a spiritual, emotional, and physical toll on ourselves and on our relationships. At these times, it might be helpful to contact a pastor, a spiritual director, a pastoral counselor, or a therapist.

It is important when dealing with shame to seek assistance from trained mental-health professionals. For help in locating a pastoral counselor, go to the Web site for the American Association of Pastoral Counselors at *aapc.org*.

New Life and God's Grace

Ultimately, God wants us to accept not only grace and responsibility but the gifts of new life. Forgiving others moves us to stronger connections to those whom we call our family, friends, or community. Forgiving ourselves becomes an opportunity to deepen our self-understanding and our experience of God's grace.

Closing Worship

Return to the story of Jessica. Reflect on your earlier thoughts about forgiveness in the story. How has your mind changed? What beliefs or attitudes have been affirmed through the lesson? How have you been challenged to think about our life through the story of Jessica? Pray silently for those who struggle daily to accept God's grace in overcoming shame and for those working the forgiveness process for wrongs they have done to themselves and to others. Close by praying together the Lord's Prayer.

Additional Resources
Agents of Hope: A Pastoral Psychology, by Donald Capps (Fortress Press, 1995).
Shame: The Power of Caring, by Gershen Kaufman (Schenkman Books, Inc., 1992).
Transforming Shame: A Pastoral Response, by Jill L. McNish (Haworth Pastoral Press, 2004).
Moving From Shame to Self-Worth: Preaching & Pastoral Care, by Edward P. Wimberly (Abingdon Press, 1999).

Notes

[1] From "Shame," by C. D. Schneider, in *Dictionary of Pastoral Care and Counseling,* edited by Rodney J. Hunter (Abingdon Press, 1990); page 1160.

[2] From *John Wesley: Holiness of Heart and Life,* by Charles Yrigoyen, Jr. (The Mission Education and Cultivation Program Department for the Women's Division, General Board of Global Ministries, 1996); page 22.

[3] From *John Wesley: Holiness of Heart and Life*; pages 20–26.

CHAPTER 6
FORGIVING CHURCHES
AND COMMUNITIES

Focus: Like other communities, churches can be places of hurt and pain. Working the process of forgiveness as a community requires steadfastness, honesty, and courage.

Gathering

Read Colossians 3:12-17. What does this text mean to the church? How difficult is it to practice such attitudes in churches and other groups? What does the Scripture suggest about God's role as we try to live as Paul suggests? Pray silently for churches and communities in conflict. Pray aloud the following prayer: "God of peace and hope, guide us in our explorations of the process of forgiveness as a church and community. Help us discover again your grace and power, and help us open ourselves to forgive one another as you forgive us. In Christ we pray. Amen."

Case Study

Paul and Gretchen have been part of the same local church for many years. They have raised their children in this church and have given much time and energy over the years to its vitality. Recently there has been a growing tension in the church around an issue of social justice. The pastor is encouraging persons to have open and honest conversation about their different perspectives. Various members in the church are claiming to have the appropriate "Christian" stance on the issue, and Paul and Gretchen find themselves approaching the issue from a very different perspective than many of their long-time friends. Conversations during church school and at the social hour often center on the conflict. They are surprised by the depth of passion people feel and are also surprised that those whom they thought they knew so well are in such different places. The conflict not only affects their social lives in the church, but they are also noticing an ongoing restlessness in their spiritual lives. At a recent meeting, Paul and Gretchen found themselves taking sides and speaking clearly about their commitments. It was obvious that their perspective was in the minority at the meeting. Harsh words were said by many around the table, and almost everyone felt personally attacked by someone else. At the end of the meeting, they prayed together the Lord's Prayer, saying, "Forgive us our sins as we forgive those who sin against us." They wonder if their community will ever be the same again.

> Read the case study. Who needs to be forgiven? For what? By whom?

As Christians, we are called to live in community with one another and to be the church together in the world. Our friendships with one another can be full and rich, particularly when others are willing to be present with us while we are struggling, going through a crisis, or experiencing profound grief and loss. The church also provides a place for us to make a difference in the world, for we know that through it we can reach out in the world in ways that are made stronger by our collective work. The pooling of our resources and the intentional work of the church promote God's mission in the world.

> What situations of conflict in your local church have disappointed you or caused pain?

At the same time, the churches we love the most can also be the sources of our deepest hurt, disappointment, or resentments. In part, this depth of pain is due to the fact that we know the church is called by God to be at work in the world, and therefore we expect more from it than we do from most other social institutions. We mistakenly assume that "being a church" means that we ought to get along with one another without conflict, and we should always be nice. When our best visions and desires for the community of faith are met with disappointment and pain, we feel angry, injured, and hurt. Churches become places of intense conflict even

70

when we so deeply desire them to embody the kind of love and care that we hope for in a community of faith.

Like other institutions and communities, churches are human and fallible. In fact, it is precisely because the church is made up of human beings trying to discern God's will that we know conflict will be present. Disagreements are sometimes even necessary, as they help us discern how best to embody God's care for the world. The church will never be perfect. What we can hope for is faithfulness in response to pain and injury through the process of forgiveness. Were it not so, there would be little need to struggle with living in community.

In this session, we will look at churches as forgiven and forgiving communities of faith. By examining what it means to live in community and to be a community engaged in the world, we will see that there are two levels at which issues of pain and hurt—as well as forgiveness—exist. The first level relates to intra-institutional conflict, while the second notes the church's connection to broader systems of injustice. From there we will turn to examine how communities of faith might practice forgiveness.

> Reflect on the history of the church over the centuries. Name places of sin and conflict in the church and occasions when people have been hurt or injured by the institution.

Sin and its counterparts of pain, hurt, and injury are operative at two levels in the church. First, the church in its humanness falls short, and sin lives within local and denominational life. Second, the church is active in the world and, as a result, participates in systemic injustices that cause harm and injury to others. While these two levels are distinct, they are connected in our daily lives in ways that are sometimes obvious while, at other times, quite hard to discern.

Local Church and Denominational Conflicts

On the first level, within all human communities—in spite of their best intentions—people experience pain and often feel wounded. The church is no exception. There may be many reasons for the hurt, and there is rarely only one person who feels the pain. Because of deep convictions of faith, we find ourselves on different sides of various issues.

Sometimes the issues are integral to the inner life of a particular community. Church members fight over decisions about how to develop the budget, allocate resources, confront pastoral leadership, or remodel the kitchen. Other times, the conflicts relate to the complexity of being part of a larger denomination. For example, we know that we are not all of one mind on many social issues that confront the church and the world. Conflict shows up both within individual congregations and within the larger denominational structures. In all of these situations, tensions either erupt quickly or sit quietly beneath the surface festering and waiting to be made known, often affecting the congregation in subtle and unconscious ways.

What are some issues that create conflict for your denomination?

In and of themselves, disagreements are not always bad. In fact, conflicts often assist us in discerning what is at stake in our conversations and deliberations. The deep passions of our faith are exhibited in the concerns and convictions that we carry into our daily lives, and it is the way that we are called to live. Differences in perspectives, interpretations of Scripture and tradition, and individual life experiences create places of dissonance and a lack of harmony. When we allow our disagreements to take shape carefully and thoughtfully, the conflict can be helpful and can assist us in discernment processes.

What are some situations in your church in which conflict or disagreements have led to positive results?

The problem is that often in the midst of our conflicts and passions, we end up intentionally and unintentionally hurting one another. We forget that our places of deep conviction may not be met favorably by our sister or brother in the faith. We allow our fear and anger to cause us to turn on one another, and we argue in ways that create barriers between ourselves and ultimately between our community and God's grace. We sin and break covenant as the church and the people of God. In moments like these, we can lean on the gift of forgiveness as one way to journey through the abyss of feelings and fears. Forgiving the church and its members—our friends and neighbors—can be a difficult process.

Return to the opening case study. Where might the covenants between one another and God have been broken?

The Church in the World

At a second level, the brokenness of the church is apparent in broader and systemic ways. We are a church that exists in a world where injustice, wars, and violence seem unending. The church cannot distance itself from larger systems and cannot deny the ways that cultural sin affects our attempts to live as holy people. Just as we know that as individuals we are sinners, so also we are aware that the systems of which we are a part perpetuate injustices and cause harm and injury to others. The church must not only work toward justice, but it must also recognize and name its own sin, asking forgiveness from those whom we have unintentionally or intentionally hurt in the process.

In the Christian community, we understand that we are corporately —not just individually—responsible for the sins in the world. We are part of larger systems and communities where relationships and covenants are broken and where corporate sin is often expressed against individuals and groups. In a classic text on justice, Iris Young suggests there are "five faces of oppression" that keep us from realizing fullness in the world: 1) exploitation of others through money and power; 2) marginalization of groups of people by denying them access to essential parts of the community; 3) the need to keep people "in their places" by denying their voices and ignoring their cries; 4) participation in the culture in ways that promote imperialism and dominance; and 5) perpetuation of violence in the world.[1]

Racism, ageism, sexism, heterosexism, global injustice, ethnic genocide, and the atrocities of war are but a few of the manifestations of such abuses in our culture. In systemic injustice and sin, it is not simply that individuals cause hurt and pain to other individuals; rather, it is that we participate in broader cultural structures that keep sin in place. We take part in promoting behaviors, attitudes, or prejudices that negatively affect others. Or, we sit silently watching oppression happen in the world around us and do not raise our prophetic voices

> Form teams of two or three. What are some of the injustices in our world that the church needs to address? Make a list. Come together as one large group and talk about your lists. Create one list for the entire group. In what ways has your church addressed issues of injustice that you have listed? How might it address any of the listed injustices?

in response. As people of faith, we cannot deny the fact that we are participants in the sins of the world.

Racism illustrates the complex nature of this communal sin and responsibility, particularly as it exists in explicit and implicit ways in our culture and in our churches. The structures of racism are held in place both by churches that promote such attitudes and prejudices as well as by ones that keep silence in the face of such systemic injustice. Bigotry and hatred are easy to identify when they are overt and direct, hopefully compelling all of us to speak out against it. More difficult to confront are the attitudes and structures that operate in covert ways, many times without our conscious awareness of them. Until we find systemic ways of holding the culture and ourselves accountable, working toward antiracism, we will be caught in the broader cultural structures that work to keep people in their respective places.

Naming and claiming our participation in structures of oppression are made more difficult by the unwillingness of those in the dominant culture to be honest about how easy it is to forget that injustice exists, simply because it does not affect the majority in the same way that it has an impact on those who are its genuine victims. While it would be true to say that racism makes everyone a victim, it is also naive to suggest that those in the dominant culture feel the oppression on a daily basis in the same way that persons of color do in the United States.

> In what ways do you see the church participating in the sin of the world?

Naming racism as something to which the church ought to respond will bring us one step closer to thinking about how forgiveness might bring greater healing and wholeness.

The church is part of the brokenness of the world. We experience the estrangement of relationships when our churches are in conflict locally or denominationally. We also participate in the perpetuation of injustice through the systemic and corporate nature of sin. To be forgiven and forgiving as a church means we must address both levels of sin.

Communal Processes of Forgiveness

The forgiveness process in community touches on many of the same movements identified in the previous sessions of this study. However, the involvement of more people along with their individual and collective histories collude to create a more cumbersome and complex process.

74

Because of the multiple relationships at work here, there is a greater potential that the process itself will result in more pain and hurt. Forgiveness takes more time, energy, and effort when more people and systems are involved in the injury, wounding, or injustice.

It is important to remember that the goal of communal forgiveness is not simply to arrive at a place where people feel better, although that will surely happen. Instead, the goal is to experience liberation and freedom in ways that engage us fully in the reign of God. As is true in individual relationships, communal forgiveness requires that we tend to the process and to the relationships involved, not simply to the outcome. The ongoing work of naming, repenting, changing, and working toward reconciliation gives us the space necessary to recognize that wholeness comes as we take smaller steps in just and loving ways. Trying to move too quickly toward resolution shortchanges the positive benefits of the process itself, which can move us toward the fullness of God's grace.

While the process of forgiveness in community is more complex, it also offers the greatest potential for systemic change, ultimately having a larger effect on more people in positive ways. If the process of forgiveness is tended to with care, there is the possibility that relationships will not only be positively affected but also that they will be strengthened in ways that will increase and strengthen our relationships with one another, with the world, and with God.

Four Components of the Communal Process of Forgiveness

Honestly Listen to Others' Pain, and Name Sins in Community

Important Elements in the Communal Processes of Forgiveness
- Honestly listen to others' pain, and name sins in community.
- Remain steadfastly present to the process.
- Discern carefully how to take action.
- Draw upon the resources of our faith and tradition.

Listening carefully to the pain of others is more difficult than we sometimes imagine. In community, it is important to remember that there are multiple voices and many experiences of one incident of injury or harm. We have to create the space and time necessary to allow all voices to be heard, even those with whom we deeply disagree. Additionally, there are times when the community has to give explicit permission to people

75

to share painful experiences and perspectives, even when it is difficult for those who hear them.

Listening requires that we pay attention not only to the strongest voices but also to those that are quiet or silent. It takes courage to listen fully to the pain of others on two counts. First, listening carefully means opening ourselves to our own hurt and realizing that the pain of others connects to ours. Second, listening fully to the pain of others sometimes requires that we change something in ourselves. In hearing the pain, we often confront our shortcomings, our lack of insight and care, or a behavior or attitude that has caused harm. It is difficult to listen fully and to take in the pain of others.

We must be careful not to scapegoat the ones who experience pain in the process. Remember that engaging the process of forgiveness will undoubtedly uncover and create new hurts. The process rarely happens smoothly or without failures. At times, some may wish that those who have been hurt would simply get over their pain so that we all could get on with

> When have you felt tempted to tell someone "Get over it!" as that person described his or her hurt?

healing. However, I believe it is not appropriate, honest, or fair to request that others simply deny their feelings or experiences just because it is too painful for the rest of us. We must be willing to allow the ones who have been hurt to work through their pain in ways with which we may not be completely comfortable. Undoubtedly there will be moments of increased tension and hurt; this is not the end of the story unless the process falters completely.

We listen to the pain of others not only to release them or ourselves from the depths of woundedness but also because we know that only by taking in the depth of hurt can we begin to discern precisely what the forgiveness is about. In a careful process, we hope that listening to the pain will release people from the grasp that hurt and anger might have on their lives. Yet, it sometimes makes us uncomfortable and can create hurt, pain, or injury in the listener. The goal is not simply to listen but also to try to gain as clear and full a picture as possible.

Living as forgiven and forgiving communities of faith involves trying to listen to multiple truths in order to move toward God's reconciliation or shalom. Naming systemic and communal sin and forgiveness requires that we recognize the interrelatedness of various structures of oppression and injustice. There is rarely one single causative factor involved in communal and corporate sin. Instead, what is more clearly the case is often that one sin or injustice is interrelated to other sins or injustices. Just as there is no single cause to corporate sin, there is also no single path to forgiveness.

As we listen to how others perceive and experience an injustice or a wrong, we can begin to "name" the sin collectively. The more a community can wrestle with the pain of all involved, the greater the chance of naming the sin in ways that are honest in the community. Once we have named the sin as a community, we can then begin to ask for forgiveness or seek forgiveness, leading us to repentance and change.

Remain Steadfastly Present to the Process

The practice of forgiveness in community requires that we remain at the table, working to keep conversation and dialogue as open and honest as possible. In and of itself, this is often a very difficult task. Remaining at the table means three things. First, we cannot abandon the process of forgiveness as a community. The process is not the work of any one or two individuals; it is the work of the whole. Hence, it is imperative that the community somehow take responsibility for the process itself.

Second, staying present to the process should not be interpreted as meaning that everyone needs to remain at the table all the time. In the process of forgiveness, there may be times when individuals or groups of people will need to absent themselves. Perhaps they have been injured in the process and need space to heal a bit before they listen once again. Or perhaps they feel abused by others in the work and need to keep a safe distance in order to return to the conversation with a sense of integrity. What is important is for all participants to respect the needs of others to be absent at times from the process. What we

> What does it mean to you and to your church to "remain at the table" when you experience disagreement and conflict in the church? What causes you or others to want to leave the table?

trust is that as a community, we are all in this together, and we all work in different and various ways throughout the process. If we cannot be physically present in a particular phase of a process, prayer can become one of the ways to remain steadfast and faithful.

Third, we must assume that others are as genuine in their Christian walk and as faithful to their call as we feel ourselves. One of the struggles in the forgiveness process is to be generous with those whom we feel have hurt us, those whom we fear are on the "wrong side," or those whom we believe not to be genuine. In order for the process to work, we must be willing to engage those who come from very different perspectives.

Discern Carefully How to Take Action

What is often required of us in cases of communal sin is not only to engage honestly and openly in conversations but eventually to take actions that create change. There are several ways to contemplate the kinds of actions that are required. First, the action may be one of repentance and seeking forgiveness from others. In local congregations, sometimes this means seeking forgiveness from or offering forgiveness to our neighbors and friends even when we continue to disagree with their perspective. In larger cultural contexts, forgiveness sometimes requires us to repent and to work toward change that may take years to effect. Transformation and movement toward reconciliation require genuine repentance on the part of all. It is not impossible to conceive that people will repent, but the amount of faithful courage required should not be underestimated.

Such action may require us to ask questions about what God would intend for those who have harmed us or for those whom we have harmed. There are times when our repentance may invoke us to change an attitude, pattern of behavior, or perspective that we have carried for a long time. In cases like this, the action may move us to grieve the loss of vision for an ideal community.

> Consider past conflicts that have been resolved in your church. What actions contributed to the resolution of the conflict? How did the process of forgiveness work in the resolution of the conflict?

Instead, we are left working to change ourselves so that we can live faithfully and steadfastly in community.

Action may also require that we reestablish covenants that have been broken. Finding ways to establish new ways of relating can take considerable time. Renegotiating the structures of our relationships with others ultimately can lead us to a renewed covenant with God.

Draw Upon the Resources of Our Faith and Tradition

As Christians, we bring to the process of forgiveness incredible resources of our faith and tradition. Theologian L. Gregory Jones notes that the sacraments of Baptism and the Lord's Supper have deep connections to forgiveness. Through them, we are reminded of the gift of God's grace in our lives. Additionally, these sacraments lead us to a renewed sense of community in Christ, reminding us that in spite of our differences, in Christ we are one.[2]

Another resource we bring to the process of forgiveness is our ability to pray, especially for those whom we do not understand, for those we are hurting, and for those who actively or unconsciously hurt us. It is in the moment of praying corporately for the other that we can appeal to God to shift and change our own perspectives. What this means, of

> Return to the opening case study. What practical steps would you take after the meeting to engage the process of forgiveness? How might the church be different because of the forgiveness process?

course, is that we genuinely have to pray for openness and change within ourselves, not simply for the other to come to new awareness or new understandings. It takes courage to pray because after all, God might call us to repent, to change, and to be transformed in the midst of our prayers.

Ultimately, living into the promise and hope of forgiveness on a daily basis has an effect on our church and world. Doing forgiveness work in our individual and corporate lives offers us the opportunity to practice both forgiving and being forgiven.

The community that works the process of forgiveness listens fully and carefully, remains steadfast to the process, takes change and action seriously, and continues to draw upon the resources of faith. When communities engage one another in the forgiveness process, they change and can never again be the same. Such processes deepen our relationships with one another, with the broader communities of which we are a part, and with God.

Closing Worship

Sing or read the hymn "The Church's One Foundation." Pray for churches in conflict and for wisdom as people engage the forgiveness process. Close the session with the Lord's Prayer.

79

Additional Resources
Embodying Forgiveness: A Theological Analysis, by L. Gregory Jones (William B. Eerdmans Publishing Company, 1995).

Notes

[1] From *Justice and the Politics of Difference,* by Iris Marion Young (Princeton University Press, 1990); pages 39–65.
[2] From *Embodying Forgiveness: A Theological Analysis,* by L. Gregory Jones (William B. Eerdmans Publishing Company, 1995); pages 163–206.

CHAPTER 7
A FORGIVING CHURCH
IN THE WORLD

Focus: As individuals and as a community of faith, God calls us to transform the world around us by living as forgiven and forgiving people.

Gathering

Greet one another. Find a partner. Talk about key ideas of the last six sessions. What have been the most significant points for you? Talk about what it means to you to be a forgiven and forgiving people. Share highlights of your conversation with the entire group. Pray aloud the following prayer: "Powerful and forgiving God, you have called us to be a church and to offer to the world a new vision for deepening our connection to ourselves, to one another, to larger communities, and ultimately to you through the process of forgiveness. Lead us as we examine ways that we can honor your gifts and ways that we can live so others will also be blessed by glimpses of wholeness and holiness. In Christ we pray. Amen."

Case Study

Holocaust survivor Simon Wiesenthal tells a gripping story about the faithful struggle to forgive. Caught in the anguish of a Nazi concentration camp, Wiesenthal is taken to the bedside of a German SS soldier who lies dying. The soldier confesses the horrors and atrocities he has committed, asking Wiesenthal for forgiveness. Wiesenthal hears the request but does not verbally respond. He returns to his friends at the camp and talks about the experience and the questions it raises. Some suggest to him that it is not up to him to forgive on behalf of the entire Jewish community. In fact, for Wiesenthal to forgive on behalf of a whole community that has been hurt seems ostentatious. Another suggests that perhaps the soldier was repenting and deserved to be pardoned as his last request before dying.

The story lives on in Wiesenthal's soul long after he is released from the concentration camp and the war ends. Wrestling with the memory of the camps and this soldier's request, Wiesenthal visits the home of the soldier who died. The mother of the soldier offers him a mother's "faith in the goodness of her son."[1] Wiesenthal never discloses who he is or the truths he knows about her son. Through the

What would you have done in Wiesenthal's place?

retelling of the story, he continues to ponder and invite others into thinking about the possibilities and limitations of forgiveness. The story ends with Wiesenthal asking those who read his story what they would have done in his situation.

The story of Simon Wiesenthal, his friends and neighbors, the soldier and his mother, the response of the rest of the world to the horror of the Holocaust, and the ongoing memories of that period in our global history raise many of the same questions with which we began this study. The goal of this study has not been to answer all of the questions but to offer new ways of thinking about an ancient truth called forgiveness. The objective here has been to offer a space and place for individuals and communities to reflect on the meaning of forgiveness in the life of Christians.

Consider what life in our world would be like if all persons and communities lived as a forgiven and forgiving people. Create a group mural by drawing or writing about this life on a large sheet of paper or poster paper. What steps can you or your church take to move toward such a vision?

Through this study, we have examined the biblical imperative to forgive and have suggested that the God who offers us forgiveness is also the one who holds us accountable for our sins. While we are certainly sinners one and all, we are not held hostage by our sins. Instead, we are offered a process that takes us through repentance and moves us toward wholeness and holiness. We are called to live as forgiven and forgiving people, trusting the God who seeks justice and reconciliation. Theologically, we have suggested that God creates us to be in right relationship. However, we break covenant with God, with one another, and with the world through our individual and corporate sin. The God who intends justice, reconciliation, and

> Read Micah 6:8. How does this Scripture inform the call to live as a forgiven and forgiving people? What actions does it suggest? What are the implications for human relationships with God and with one another?

wholeness for all people and communities offers forgiveness as a means to a holy way of life.

The process of forgiveness is multilayered and often does not occur smoothly or effortlessly. The movements in the process take us from the time in which a hurt, injustice, or injury is inflicted to the time of reconciliation. There are at least three things that hinder the process of forgiveness. When we revert to cycles of blame and shame, when we are unable to name or claim feelings, or when we lack sufficient community around us, the path of forgiveness becomes cumbersome and alienating rather than liberating and healing. On the other hand, the qualities of mutuality, honesty, the ability to listen deeply and fully, patience, and steadfastness all give us the grace we need to be able to pray God's best intentions for others and to work the process of forgiveness.

Forgiveness of the self requires that we separate our sense of shame from genuine and honest feelings of guilt. The former aspect, our shame, is an internal lack of self-worth. Shame blocks us from experiencing any sense of grace. While guilt also blocks us from grace, it is an appropriate response to things we have done wrong. Addressing our guilt through the process of forgiveness involves taking self-inventory, acknowledging our wrongdoing, asking for forgiveness, practicing genuine repentance and change, and remaining engaged and in dialogue with others.

Living in community naturally means that we will experience hurt, disappointment, and anger from time to time. While the forgiveness process in the context of community is sometimes cumbersome and labor-intensive, it can free us to restore relationships with friends, neighbors, denominations, and even larger communities. The process of forgiveness in community may extend over generations in some cases, yet in spite of the energy and time required, it is a process that can bring healing and wholeness to the church and to the world.

Three Commitments

In the end, forgiveness stands as a central understanding of our Christian faith. How then can we move into the world in ways that reflect the power and call of forgiveness in our lives? There are three commitments in living the holy life of forgiveness that encourage us to move beyond this study and to practice forgiveness in the world. First, we must be committed to face the questions of our lives without fearing that they will compromise our faith. Second, the church needs to continue its commitment to teach our children about forgiveness through our thoughts, words, stories, and deeds. Third, as God calls us to be the church in the world, we are committed to live as forgiven and forgiving people who work for justice and liberation on behalf of others and of the world. The process of forgiveness can change the world in which we live.

Moving Beyond This Study
- Live into the questions.
- Teach our children.
- Work for justice in the world.

Live Into the Questions

Much like Wiesenthal's story, this study leaves us with unanswered questions. What do we do when we are called to forgive others and are not yet ready or prepared to do so? How do we discern the motives of someone's petition of forgiveness, confession, or words of repentance? Are the motives even important to the process? What if God is the one whom someone feels the need to forgive? Are there some atrocities that can never be forgiven? Can individuals forgive on behalf of a larger community? When confronting larger global issues, how do we maintain the process of forgiveness for the sake of genuine repentance and change? Can forgiveness work in global politics? When the answers seem less than clear, wrestling with questions like these can deepen our spiritual and faith life and our relationship with God.

Questions are important to the life of faith but not simply for the sake of the questions themselves. Instead, their usefulness is that they allow us to open ourselves to the spirit of God moving in ways that we might not have predicted. Questions help us determine the parameters of our beliefs, and they guide us toward action. They offer us new avenues to explore, and they can deepen our convictions about our faith. The goal of exploring our faith is not simply to arrive at pleasant platitudes for people to hold on to in distress; rather, it is to provide meaningful stability and hope in the midst of life's chaos. Through good, vibrant questions, we gain deeper insight into what it means to live as faithful Christians in the world. Questions about forgiveness engage our minds and souls in ways that give us a greater ability to see God's presence in the world around us.

> Form teams of two or three, and discuss the questions in the first paragraph of "Live Into the Questions." How would you answer one or more of these questions? What is challenging about them? How does wrestling with the questions inform or affect your faith life or your relationship with God?

There are questions that startle us at times and may even raise conflicts about our beliefs. A question that disturbs some Christians is wondering how to forgive God. The subject raises other questions about the power and limitation of God's activity in the world. Even when we believe in a God of power, there are still times when we experience the unfairness or injustice of life and wonder how God could allow such things to happen to us or to those we love. We wonder why God doesn't change the outcomes for some but seems to change them for others. These questions are the matters of our deepest struggles and deserve our ongoing attention. They should not leave us faithless; the wrestling should leave us stronger, even in light of answers that feel distant.

What seems clear is that God does not mind us asking questions about faith or about the role of the Holy One in our lives. If God were threatened by the depths of our minds and souls, we would not be given the words of the psalmists, who often lament aloud wondering where God is while the world around them crumbles (Psalm 13, Psalm 142). They remind us that God hears our cries and perhaps even cries with us. In the end, the one who voices lament is reminded that God has been faithful through the ages and will continue to be so for the future.

> Read Psalm 13 and Psalm 142. What do these psalms say to you about God? About humans? How might such psalms help you as you struggle with God's role in the process of forgiveness?

God is not to blame for our misfortunes, and some would suggest that God does not need to be forgiven. But we need not protect God from those moments when we feel incredible pain and anger toward God for not intervening in our lives in ways that we imagine would create less pain and trauma for us. God can handle our emotions, our questions, and our fears. God's response to our perplexity is found in the story of Exodus 3. As Moses encounters God on the mountain and is told to go and lead the people, Moses asks, "Who am I that I should go to Pharaoh, and bring the Israelites out of Egypt?" God responds simply by saying, "I will be with you" (vv. 11-12). The promise to Moses—and to us—is not for an easy or painless journey but for a faithful and present God who lives with us through the depths of our struggles.

Questions about forgiveness will continue to live in our souls. By our ability to articulate the depth of our concerns to one another and to the world, we also illustrate to others that the Holy One cares for us enough to grace us with minds, hearts, and souls that struggle faithfully with such issues as forgiveness. The world around us is changed as the church dares to ask questions of itself. Those beyond the walls of the church come to see and know through us that our God is big enough to hold all of us in grace without fail. Indeed, this is good and transforming news for the world.

> What questions remain for you about the process of forgiveness? About the potential of living as a forgiven and forgiving people?

Teach Our Children

A second way to move beyond this study is to teach our children, through actions and stories, what it means to be a forgiven and forgiving church in the world. We can do this in a number of ways. For example, embracing our liturgical and ritual life as a community reminds children on a weekly basis about the courage of the church to name sins, to ask for forgiveness, to receive sacraments of grace, and to live holy lives. Teaching children how to be honest about shortcomings and failures is not an insignificant gift to them or to the world. When children know that it is all right to ask for forgiveness, to repent, and to change their ways—even in very small and incremental steps—we are teaching them about forgiveness.

Prayer and spiritual life are important in the forgiveness process. Children learn how to pray by doing it with us daily and weekly in church. They need to realize that there are times when we can only voice our deepest fears, angers, hurts, and wrongs to God in the form of a silent prayer, and this is acceptable in God's sight. As children participate in worship where prayers of confession and words of assurance are said aloud and often, they learn that it is good and honorable to come before God with a clean and pure heart. Reflecting on his journeys in churches in South Africa, Desmond Tutu once commented that "a prayed-in church is qualitatively different from one that has the atmosphere of a concert hall."[2] Our children need to know what it feels like to be in a community of faith that believes in the power of prayer, even when there are no quick answers. They deserve not only to know the words of the Lord's Prayer but also to experience people who honestly believe that we can forgive others, just as we can name our sins to God and ask for forgiveness.

> Locate a prayer of confession and words of assurance in your church's worship resources. Read these in your group. What do they say to you about the way worship supports the process of forgiveness?

Many churches have developed a time to greet their neighbors and friends during the opening moments of worship or at some point during the service itself. This has been linked to the tradition of "passing the peace." This ancient ritual of reaching out to one another in the name of God and offering others the peace of Christ that comes from knowing we are forgiven people invites us to sit at the table with those with whom we have deep disagreements or those against whom we harbor negative feelings. At the same time, passing the peace encourages us to live in the world as faithful Christians who share acts of forgiveness with others, even when we may not feel like it. As forgiven people, we reach out in forgiveness and in peace to one another. Our children deserve to see adults who act with loving kindness and grace toward one another. In recognizing the importance of greeting one another in the name of Christ, we also claim God's forgiving power in the neighbor whom we have wronged or who we feel has wronged us.

Teaching children that it is good to ask for help and assistance is an invaluable lesson for us all. As we know, there are times when the journey of forgiveness feels long and lonely. Friends, neighbors, family members, and pastors can be helpful partners in our journey. We need to continue to teach children how to be in covenantal relationships with those around them so that they value relationships as gifts of God. Likewise, it is important to help children (and sometimes adults) learn that it is all right to ask for professional help when we feel the journey is too painful or too difficult. Trained pastoral counselors and other therapists can become invaluable resources to individuals and to the community as we struggle with the vulnerabilities and pains of our lives.

We live in an intergenerational community where we can both pass on the gifts of our faith as well as teach our children and others about living that faith in the world. L. Gregory Jones suggests that "forgiveness must be embodied in specific habits and practices of Christian life,

> What would you like to teach the children of your church about forgiveness? How will you make that happen?

paradigmatically as we become part of Christ's Body, the Church. Learning to embody forgiveness involves our commitment to the cultivation of specific habits and practices of the Church.... There is a craft of forgiveness that Christians are called to learn from one another, and particularly from exemplars, as we seek to become holy people."[3] We are called to teach our children about the craft of forgiveness by being their exemplars of holy living.

Work for Justice in the World

God has a mission for the church in the world. The intent of God is to establish a reign where justice, liberation, and wholeness are present for everyone and everything in creation. Forgiveness is one part of that larger vision to which God calls the church. As the church, we gather as a human community where we know that we have transgressed and caused harm to others, consciously or unconsciously. At the same time, as the gathered church, we believe we are forgiven and are called to work steadfastly on behalf of others. We are to offer the world forgiveness as one option in response to the pain and suffering we experience in our

> How is your church at work for justice in the world?

individual, familial, and community lives. The church carries the good news into the world through its actions and reflections.

Gary Gunderson, author and director of the Interfaith Health Program of the Carter Center, maintains that the power of communities of faith rests in eight specific strengths that they pass on to their members and to those around them. The church becomes a place where we accompany one another, convene, connect, tell stories, give sanctuary, bless, pray, and endure.[4] As the church gathers together to participate in these activities for ourselves, we also gather on behalf of the world and are empowered to move into the world telling the stories of the faith. We know that it is not enough simply to hang on to the gospel for ourselves; we are called to take the good news to others. Through processes of forgiveness in our communities, we offer the world an alternative to violence and hatred.

As a part of that call, we are given the mandate to live as a forgiven community, believing that God is already at work. There are three ways we have a broader impact on the world as we participate in the work of forgiveness.

> **Three Ways to Be the Church in the World**
> - Solidarity with the most vulnerable
> - Truth-telling from various perspectives
> - Patience with the process

First, the church is called to remain in solidarity with those who are most vulnerable in the world. It stands with those who have less to offer, who have been recipients of an injustice, who are poor, or who remain marginalized in the world. To stand with them means to recognize that injustices and harms have been done that affect not only their lives but all of creation as well. We are connected one to another. Such awareness leads us to participate in acts of repentance and change and to invite forgiveness when we see it needed in the world around us. As people of faith, we remain steadfast with others, not giving up when the pain is too much to bear. Instead, we believe that the power of forgiveness and the grace of God can transform the world, especially for the most vulnerable.

Second, we must allow for truths to be told, even when they are painful to hear or when they incriminate us in some way. Truth-telling is very difficult, and sometimes it is also a very dangerous activity. To speak truths invites us to consider the wrongs we have done and to be honest about our complicity or culpability in the sins of the world. As a part of this truth-telling, we are aware that different people will see things from unique perspectives. The particularities lead to differences that need to be honored, not dismissed. There is not one singular truth, and we must listen for the way that God speaks in multiple voices and in multiple ways. Honoring multiple expressions of truth sets us free to explore forgiveness and reconciliation in new and surprising ways.

Third, the church must encourage patience with the process of forgiveness at individual, communal, and global levels. Between individuals and families, the process changes the lives of the individuals and the dynamics of all the relationships in which we are involved. Even as these good changes occur, chaos emerges as people struggle with new ways of relating to one another. The same is true on the larger communal levels. As churches embody the craft of forgiveness, they will change the way that they relate to one another. If the world embraces processes of forgiveness, it will change the global climate in ways that will bring us ever closer to the reign of God on earth.

Forgiveness: A Gift From God

Forgiveness is a gift from God, offered not only to those of us in the church but also to the world. As we practice the craft of forgiveness in our individual lives and in the lives of our churches, we offer the world a new vision for deepening our connection to ourselves, to one another, to larger communities, and ultimately to God. We are deeply blessed by this gift of forgiveness because it offers us glimpses of wholeness and holiness.

Closing Prayer
Sing or read aloud the hymn "What Does the Lord Require" or another favorite hymn about social holiness, such as "For the Healing of the Nations," "Jesus, Jesu," or "Let There Be Peace on Earth." Pray silently about your life individually and as a community. Where are the places to practice being a forgiven and forgiving people? Close the session by praying together the Lord's Prayer.

Additional Resources
Deeply Woven Roots: Improving the Quality of Life in Your Community, by Gary Gunderson (Fortress Press, 1997).
The Sunflower: On the Possibilities and Limits of Forgiveness, by Simon Wiesenthal (Shocken Books, 1997).

Notes

[1] From *The Sunflower: On the Possibilities and Limits of Forgiveness,* by Simon Wiesenthal (Shocken Books, 1997); page 94.

[2] From *No Future Without Forgiveness*, by Desmond Mpilo Tutu (Doubleday, 1999); page 263.

[3] From *Embodying Forgiveness: A Theological Analysis*, by L. Gregory Jones (William B. Eerdmans Publishing Company, 1995); page xii.

[4] From *Deeply Woven Roots: Improving the Quality of Life in Your Community*, by Gary Gunderson (Fortress Press, 1997).